The Persistent Pianist

The Persistent Pianist

A BOOK FOR
THE LATE BEGINNER AND
ADULT RE-STARTER

EILEEN D. ROBILLIARD

with a Preface by Reginald Jevons

London
OXFORD UNIVERSITY PRESS
NEW YORK TORONTO

Oxford University Press, Ely House, London W.1

GLASGOW NEW YORK TORONTO MELBOURNE WELLINGTON
CAPE TOWN SALISBURY IBADAN NAIROBI LUSAKA ADDIS ABABA
BOMBAY CALCUTTA MADRAS KARACHI LAHORE DACCA
KUALA LUMPUR SINGAPORE HONG KONG TOKYO

© Oxford University Press 1967

First published 1967

Reprinted 1968

16453

786.3

Printed in Great Britain by
Butler & Tanner Ltd, Frome and London

'Failure only begins when you leave off trying to succeed.'

Preface

IN the field of education for leisure (or pleasure) the student of the piano is often less concerned with problems of learning than with fears and anxieties which seem to beset his path. Tremulously he persists in his studies, yet he is filled with doubts which not only retard his progress but induce despair in his teacher.

Of course there are books and methods galore, including the 'Teach Yourself' variety, giving all the necessary technical information, but the psychological problems, which create the chief obstacles to success for this type of student, have as yet received little attention. Certainly the experienced piano teacher has a few stock answers to the anxious questions raised by the late beginner, but disposition and personal background are so important that the proper assessment of them may make the difference between success or failure.

A large number of adults reach a stage when they feel that the practice of music in some form or other could fill a gap in their lives. That there is more than a little truth in this idea has been proved over and over again. In nearly forty years of musical activity in Further Education I have met a great number of people, from all walks of life, whose modest efforts at the piano have given them untold joy and satisfaction and even helped in overcoming mental and physical illnesses.

Eileen Robilliard's book is about psychological fears and ills experienced by amateur pianists of all ages and varying musical ability. She examines and analyses various case-histories, and makes helpful practical suggestions with regard to technical problems and graded repertoire. With luck, judgement, *and this book* a persistent pianist could go far along the pianistic road. In short, the book is a valuable contribution to this neglected field of study-help and offers much needed enlightenment to the thousands who play the piano for pleasure.

REGINALD JEVONS

Contents

Author's Foreword

THIS book may be described as an optimistic study of the amateur pianist, with special regard to the problems and prospects of the late beginner and adult re-starter at the piano.

The idea was conceived more than four years ago when a sudden period of enforced leisure, occasioned by an acute and protracted attack of lumbago, provided me with the time in which to reconsider some of the problems I had encountered daily as a private teacher of the pianoforte.

Amongst these was what writers called 'The Problem of the Adult Beginner'. That a problem existed, all seemed willing to concede. 'Every teacher has experienced disheartening attempts with adult pianoforte pupils,' wrote the late W. Gillies Whittaker.[1] But, apart from a recommendation to avoid giving adults pieces bearing childish titles, the statement that there was 'not much hope of adults making any progress in the sense of attaining agility and brilliance', together with the reminder that those who teach the teachers are primarily concerned with the needs of children, I did not come across either a clear assessment of the problem or methods of solving it.

I was not, however, prepared to accept that the problem was insoluble. I did not believe that because muscles were stiff they could not be loosened and coaxed into useful activity, nor that because brains had, in Bacon's words, 'suffered themselves to fix' they could no longer 'take the ply'. It seemed to me that the problem was not physiological but psychological. It was largely a matter of lack of confidence and lack of the right incentives.

That was what I believed. But I still wanted to know the truth. Was there any point in someone starting to take piano lessons at the age of fifty? Since I held piano-playing to be of considerable therapeutic value, quite apart from the aesthetic satisfaction it afforded, I settled down to as thorough a research as could be achieved by an

[1] In *Musical Education* (Hinrichsen, 1946).

individual working without either financial backing or the support of any recognized institution. The wonderful response which I received from almost a hundred other teachers and amateur pianists from the British Isles, New Zealand, and (a few) from America, heartened me and justified me in my undertaking.

My book is dedicated in very real gratitude to all those delightful people who became such willing 'guinea-pigs' by answering my questionnaire and writing to me. It was these people who made the task not only possible but worth while.

E. D. R.

Note: Where it is used in this book, the term 'adult beginner' must be taken to include the adult re-starter.

Acknowledgements

My sincere thanks are due to:

Miss Grace Barrons Richardson, M.A., A.R.C.M., Secretary, the Standing Conference for Amateur Music, for suggesting a number of helpful contacts.

Denis H. R. Brearley, Secretary, The Incorporated Society of Musicians, for very kindly suggesting the names of many private pianoforte teachers willing to co-operate in the research.

J. W. Miller, A.C.I.S., R.M.T., Registrar, Music Teachers' Registration Board of New Zealand, who undertook to contact the secretaries of all the local societies of registered teachers in New Zealand on my behalf.

Miss Mary Ibberson, O.B.E., founder of The Rural Music Schools Association; Miss Cicely Card, L.R.A.M., Director, Hampshire Rural Music School; Miss Yvonne Enoch, Asst. Director, Kent Rural Music School; and the County Music Advisers of Cornwall Education Committee, Gloucestershire Community Council, Somerset Rural Community Council, Staffordshire County Council Education Committee, and West Sussex County Council Education Dept. for their helpful co-operation.

J. Hindley, Asst. Education Officer, Cadbury Bros. Ltd, Bournville, Birmingham, for obtaining, through Cadbury's Works Council, amateur pianist volunteers to assist in the research.

John Clegg, concert pianist, for putting me in touch with a number of interested Music Clubs and Societies.

Reginald Jevons, Music Supervisor, Dept. of Adult Education, Goldsmiths' College, University of London, for encouraging me at the outset, and for writing the Preface to the completed work.

H. Lowery, M.Ed., Ph.D., D.Sc., F.T.C.L., for reading and approving the work when in typescript.

Maurice Jacobson, B.Mus., A.R.C.M., Hon.A.R.C.M., F.T.S.C., for his very kindly interest and advice.

J. Curwen & Sons Ltd, for supplying specimen copies of pianoforte music from their catalogue.

Alfred Lengnick & Co. Ltd, for the loan of copies of contemporary pianoforte music from their catalogue.

Pianophone Tuition Ltd, and the late James Ching, M.A., B.Mus. (Oxon), F.R.C.O., for the loan of 'The Pianist's Home Study Courses'.

I

Be Positive

'They conquer who believe they can' (Emerson)

'PEOPLE are defeated in life, not because of lack of ability, but for lack of wholeheartedness. They do not wholeheartedly expect to succeed.'[1] Among adult amateur pianists this major cause of failure —lack of belief in the likelihood of success—often goes unrecognized for the cancer it is.

The would-be pianist has to contend with many distractions: 'stiff muscles', lack of time for practice, tiredness after a day's work, household chores that demand attention, and friends who call in unexpectedly. These conceal the true cause of his slow progress, which is his basic feeling of inadequacy. He falls back on these subsidiary factors as excuses (genuine enough in themselves), not realizing that they can all be dealt with systematically and intelligently, once he has introduced the catalyst of belief into his system.

'As a man thinketh in his heart, so is he,' is as true of piano-playing as of character in general. Unconscious feelings of inadequacy, if left disregarded, will inevitably produce a thoroughly impotent pianist.

But strangely enough, there also exists the type of person who holds at subconscious levels an inflated conception of his powers. He will suffer the more acutely of the two. Whereas the first will probably finally content himself with a dilettante approach, and settle down fairly happily into an 'old dog that cannot be taught any new tricks', the second is more likely to be driven compulsively to bouts of anxiety-ridden onslaughts on technique, coupled with firm but unavailing resolutions for strictly scheduled practice

[1] Norman Vincent Peale, *The Power of Positive Thinking* (The World's Work).

periods. From all of this he will derive little or no pleasure, though most educationists would agree that in learning anything we ought to gain some satisfaction, if not also a little fun!

The amateur pianist should enjoy his piano playing: too often he does not do so.

'An adult piano pupil who has been having lessons for the past ten months . . . finds it difficult to locate intervals correctly when playing hands together,' wrote a piano teacher to a professional journal, 'and after playing one or two wrong notes *"goes to pieces" with nervousness.*'

'Perhaps you would kindly give me guidance as to suitable music and treatment for a married lady who has been with me as a pianoforte re-starter for about six months,' wrote another. 'She is keen but is *rather easily discouraged.*'

The third excerpt may be regarded as a classic case: 'I have a pupil aged 30 who has had lessons off and on with a succession of teachers since about 1945[1] with little success. She has been with me for two years . . . (and) is unable to play even a simple piece after weeks of practice. I feel sure she may be setting up a barrier between herself and the music in some way, as she *is constantly saying "I can't do it"* throughout the lesson, and plays in a stiff, tensed way despite my efforts to get her into a more relaxed frame of mind.'[2] (My italics)

One is reminded of Emile Coué's words: 'If you persuade yourself that you can do a certain thing, provided that thing be possible, you will do it, however difficult it may be. If, on the contrary, you imagine that you cannot do the simplest thing in the world, it is impossible for you to do it, and molehills become for you unscaleable mountains.'

I believe that not only does an individual's expectation of success strongly determine his ultimate achievement, but the expectations of those who are associated with him (his teacher and, to a lesser extent, his friends and relatives) also exert an influence on him. Further they will so influence him whether he be conscious of them or not! In other words, I believe that a kind of 'psychical transference' of the subjective attitudes of other persons will contribute towards his success or failure.

[1] Written in 1959.   [2] *The Music Teacher.*

This is not the expression of an atavistic belief in witchcraft, but the statement of a phenomenon that may well be scientifically valid.

In 'A New Look at the Mind',[1] Arthur Koestler, describing some of the latest experiments in American psychological research, says: 'That suggestion and auto-suggestion play a considerable part in any form of therapy is not new. What is new is that this part is incomparably more important than the physicians, and even psychiatrists, of the age of reason ever dreamed.'

'At a conservative estimate,' he notes, 'about one third of patients in any hospital ward . . . will respond to dummy pills as if they were what they believe them to be. . . . As a result, clinicians now tend to adopt the "double blind method" where the nurses themselves do not know whether they are handing out the drug or the dummy, *to eliminate unconscious suggestion*.' (My italics) We would do well, therefore, not to disregard the existence of this phenomenon.

It would seem expedient for the would-be pianist to set about finding the kind of teacher who, by seeing all his geese as potential swans, tends to produce more than his fair share of the latter. A teacher, in fact, whose own confident expectation of his pupil's success will produce just that combination of confidence, enthusiasm and inspiration most likely to ensure it.

Further, the student pianist should seek out friends or relatives who are sympathetic towards his pianistic ambitions. That this source of encouragement is not always forthcoming can be illustrated from the following replies to my questionnaire:

'*Friends and relatives mostly showed ill-concealed scorn and incredulity* at my taking up the piano—with a few notable exceptions, who showed active encouragement and even admiration.'

'My husband encourages me. *My mother-in-law thinks I waste my time*. Most of my acquaintances wonder how I find time and why I bother, when there is the wireless or television to watch.'

The general picture, however, was heartening, and the three following replies were typical:

'The attitude of my family and friends to me as an adult re-starter is one of interest, encouragement (particularly where my compositions are concerned) and constructive criticism.'

[1] *The Observer*, 23 April 1961.

'All my friends are very interested in my progress and do all they can to help and encourage me.'

'My fiancé and closest friends enjoy listening to me playing well-known classics. They encourage me to start again in earnest.'

Having gained the goodwill and encouragement of his friends and relatives, the aspiring pianist should then take steps to *get himself into a situation in which he is expected to succeed. A situation, in fact, in which his ability to play the piano is taken for granted.* He should make opportunities to play for others music that is well within his present standard of accomplishment.

For example, he might offer to play the hymns at a Sunday school or a religious group with which he has some connection. A mother might play simple nursery rhymes, Christmas Carols or 'Noddy' songs, etc.,[1] for a children's party at her home. A player who is more advanced can sometimes get the chance of performing to an audience at a local music club—particularly at a 'Members' Concert', when the platform is handed over to performer members instead of to a visiting artist. If he belongs to a choir, they may be glad of his services should the usual accompanist be absent from a practice. There are frequent opportunities for accompanying at local music festivals, especially when an official accompanist is not provided. Instrumental teachers who are unable to accompany their own pupils on the piano may welcome his help; while there are many adult competitors in the vocal classes who are often glad to find an accompanist who will rehearse with them and help them to learn the 'piano part' of their songs.

If the amateur pianist, after all his careful preparation, is suddenly attacked by last-minute 'nerves' at the public performance, he has merely to adopt the simple expedient of *acting as though he were completely confident.*

The philosopher, William James, said: 'Action seems to follow feeling, but really action and feeling go together; and by regulating the action, which is under the more direct control of the will, we can indirectly regulate the feeling, which is not. Thus the sovereign voluntary path to cheerfulness, if our spontaneous cheerfulness be lost, is to sit up cheerfully and to act and speak as if cheerfulness

[1] See Appendix 2, section 6 (p. 87): Repertoire: For Mothers and Fathers to play to their children.

were already there. If such conduct does not make you feel cheerful, nothing else on that occasion can.'

'To feel brave, act as if you were brave. Use all of your will to that end, and courage will very likely replace fear.'

The amateur pianist who has adopted a positive approach to his playing will have taken the first sure step along the road to success.

2

Setting Your Sights

> 'The fool thinks everything is easy, and comes in for many rude awakenings. The sluggard believes all is impossible, and undertakes nothing. The good workman knows that great things are possible, and, prudently, little by little, accomplishes them.' (André Maurois, *The Art of Living*)

SOMEONE who takes up amateur dramatics does so for his own enjoyment, as a means of expressing himself through developing a latent talent, and possibly also to enhance his self-esteem. Very frequently he achieves these objectives. If he admires the acting of Sir Laurence Olivier, he does not seriously expect that his own efforts will be comparable. He does not buy a record of Sir Laurence declaiming 'To be, or not to be', and make of it a yardstick with which to measure his own shortcomings. No, he rehearses diligently the part that has been allotted to him, however small it may be, and looks forward eagerly to the first night.

Some amateur pianists, however, go out and buy a record of Richter playing the Liszt *Transcendental Studies*, and then torment themselves by making comparisons with their own clumsy renderings. This type of amateur is not a 'positive pianist': he is an irrational idealist.

'Matters such as standards, both in material and in performance, must be faced with frankness and without fear, not in any narrow comparison with professional standards, because that would be a basic error. Amateur accomplishment at its finest may thrill and delight us, within its own limits. Performance on a professional platform must be judged by different criteria. It is not easy to define the differences in exact terms. In the main, all music-making sees its ultimate end in performance. To the professional, this means a presentation of a highly specialized skill and understanding in music. To the amateur it is more akin to asking an audience to share an enthusiasm for a particular kind of music.'[1] Apart from the fact that a professional's whole life is devoted to the pursuit of his art, the amateur would do well to remind himself that on a record he is not in fact hearing a true performance. In most cases he is hearing the final synthesis of an efficient system of re-recording and tape-joining of fragments from an indefinite number of performances.

The advanced amateur performer, who has been successful in competitive festival work, is often tempted to turn professional. Let us, therefore, see what are the prospects of the professional performer in this country. Quite apart from the very hard work involved in the acquisition, retention, and maintenance of professional skill, and the constant pressure of competition in a strictly limited field, the opportunities and rewards of the professional musician in this country compare unfavourably with those obtaining in other European countries today. Mr Hardie Ratcliffe, Secretary of the Musicians' Union, said in November 1960:[2]

'The more promising of the young instrumentalists and singers who emerge from training can hope for an appearance with an orchestra, or in a mixed programme, in London or elsewhere, within five years. The process of giving a Wigmore Hall recital in the hope of attracting Press notice is an expensive and often disappointing one.' (It costs at least £120.)

'During the early years the young soloist must hope to gain experience in music clubs, small provincial societies, schools and other modest ways. The fees will be very small, and concert-giving cannot at this period be regarded as a main source of livelihood. A few who have won competitions here or abroad, or secured spectacular successes in some other way, may be luckier, and can expect engagements in greater numbers. . . . Our system at present caters, in theory at least, for a limited number of first class players: it does not provide for those of more modest but adequate talent, who should have their place in any well-ordered system.'

Unless he is a performer of quite exceptional promise—and such performers are very rare indeed—the amateur should avoid the

---

[1] Sydney Northcote, *Making Your Own Music* (Phoenix, 1960).
[2] Reporting at the National Music Council Conference.

temptation of seeing himself as a professional *manqué* and should glory instead in his humbler, but just as exciting, rôle as a *lover* of music. 'There is a long and honourable tradition of amateur music-making in this country. Indeed, it may claim to be the main and most enduring feature of our musical life. Even the changing circumstances of history have failed to disturb its fundamental strength and, without it, the publishing houses, the music trades and the bulk of the musical profession could not exist. *In no art is the amateur more important than in music.*'[1]

Paul Hindemith, in *A Composer's World*,[2] acknowledges this indebtedness: 'The amateur, having always been a considerable factor in musical life, reached the climax of his importance in the eighteenth and nineteenth centuries. Our classical literature is unthinkable without the amateur in the background. He played in the orchestras together with the professional, he sang in the choirs, and for him all chamber music was written. Haydn's, Mozart's and Beethoven's quartets, even Brahms's chamber music, counted mostly on the amateur.'

But if the amateur of today is to achieve a standard of performance *acceptable to himself*, both emotionally and intellectually, he must adjust his sights to standards of achievement that fit his individual circumstances, bearing in mind the possibility of adopting improved methods of study and practice, and also what other amateurs have achieved in like circumstances.

He should not attempt to imitate the professional's technical virtuosity, nor invite frustration by attempting works that are far beyond his present standard. It is good, on occasion, to stretch oneself technically. The Chopin *Revolutionary Study*, for example, is a fine technical exercise even when taken at a slightly slower pace. One should not, however, do this sort of thing so frequently as to deserve the criticism:

> His skill is so scanty
> He plays it andante!

It is far better to devote limited practice-time to works that will

[1] *Music and the Amateur* (The National Council of Social Service, 1951).
[2] Anchor Books.

eventually yield to persistent efforts. In Appendix 2 lists of such works may be found.

The development of a deep musical understanding of music that is played will yield much more lasting satisfaction than the pursuit of technical skill for its own sake. This pursuit, indeed, is needless, since even the moderately skilled pianist can get deep and lasting enjoyment from music that is well within his limited technical capacity.

He may find it useful to keep a *Progress Diary*. In this, he should record the date on which he begins a new work, the amount of practice time that he hopes to give to it, the grade of difficulty of the work, and, finally, the total length of time that he does, in fact, spend on it before he can truly claim it as part of his repertoire. He must also set aside a certain amount of time to revise it at a later date.

He can also record his progress in acquiring technical drills, scales, arpeggios, and so on. After allowing a convenient period for the data to accumulate, he should analyse them, and set himself new targets for the future that will now have some relevance to his own past rate of progress. Such a record will act as a powerful stimulus to renewed effort, for 'learning to play an instrument or to sing proceeds with the greatest effectiveness when the individual periodically is provided with clear knowledge of progress made towards his goal. . . . In the absence of such knowledge motivation declines rapidly in strength.'[1]

Should he wish to measure his own achievements against those of other amateur pianists, he will find some standards for comparison in Chapter 7. But if he does not quite measure up to some of the best of the cases quoted, he can console himself with the thought that:

> 'To travel hopefully is a better thing than to arrive
> And the true success is to labour.'

[1] Louis P. Thorpe in *Basic Concepts in Music Education* (University of Chicago Press, 1958), p. 192.

3

Why *play* the Piano?

'To have loved the best, and to have known it for the best,
is to have been successful in life.' (Professor Mackail)[1]

'THEY laughed at first, but when I began to play, a hush fell upon
the room. I played the first few bars of Beethoven's immortal
Moonlight Sonata. My friends sat spellbound.'

We may dismiss this type of advertisement as a naïve appeal to
the exhibitionist. But fundamentally everyone wants to feel important in some way. Such a desire—like other basic needs—is
neither good nor bad in itself: only in our choice of the means for
satisfying it can we be judged. We may not attack our fellow men,
for example, but we can attack our pianistic problems. In both
cases we are satisfying our feeling for power through aggression.

However, we must beware of certain unconscious motives which
may lead us to play the piano. If they constitute the mainspring for
our pianistic activities (to the exclusion even of appreciation and love
of music itself) they may also force us to pursue, at unconscious
levels, failure rather than success. The late James Ching gives an
interesting Freudian approach to these problems in his book
Performer and Audience:[2]

'The most subtle form of conflict . . . occurs . . . when both "I
wish" and "I ought not" are overlaid, as it were, by unconscious
drives. Let us consider an example. Supposing that consciously I
wish to become a successful pianist. That, on the face of it would
seem to be a perfectly legitimate wish. But suppose that, under-
neath my *conscious* desire to become a good pianist, is the *unconscious* desire to prove myself omnipotent, to prove that I am so much

---

[1] Quoted by Percy C. Buck, *Psychology for Musicians* (Oxford University Press, 1944), p. 98.   [2] Hall the Publisher, 1947.

more clever, more gifted than anyone else in the world. In that case my super-ego will begin to say "I ought not" because all my early training will have stressed the fact that these omnipotent phantasies were "dangerous".'

'As a result, a conflict will be taking place in my Unconscious, between my super-ego and these primitive desires *without my being in any sense aware of it*. All I shall know is that an apparently innocent desire to distinguish myself as a pianist is somehow a thing liable to arouse within me feelings of intense anxiety and nervousness so that, quite inexplicably as it seems, I am never able to do myself justice, nor am I ever able to enjoy any success which I may achieve.'

He concludes: 'The task of the pianist who wishes to be able to play successfully to others is therefore to try to understand as fully as possible his own individual, unconscious personality. For it is only by understanding our unconscious motives that we can either eliminate them or lessen the distressing or disastrous results which they inflict on our achievements and our happiness.' Indeed he goes so far as to recommend a course of psycho-analysis for pianists who suspect they may be grappling with complex psychological problems.

Even if, however, we are not wallowing in the quagmire of some deep neurosis, we ought at least to examine some of our *conscious motives* for taking up piano-playing. Some years ago I was approached by a lady who wanted to improve her playing. When, after some time, it had become apparent that her progress did not equal her concern for improvement I was not surprised to learn her real reason for taking lessons. Her husband had recently acquired a 'lady friend' to whose other attractions was added that of piano-playing of a high order. And my pupil was making the mistake of trying to compete with this rival partly on her own ground!

The understandable anxiety that underlay her attempt to improve her own playing was sufficient to doom that attempt to failure. For the 'competitive element', often by itself a cause of disability, in this case carried with it all the overtones of a situation involving the 'self' in a very fundamental way: a situation which threatened attack on her 'security' in an actual as well as an emotional sense.

This case may well strike the reader as being somewhat exceptional. It is all the more pertinent to recall, therefore, that during the eighteenth and nineteenth centuries pianistic skill was foremost amongst those 'accomplishments' deemed necessary for attracting a mate, and thereby a place in 'society'.

In her *Practical Education* (1798), Maria Edgeworth makes an imaginary lady of fashion say: 'I would give anything to have my daughter play better than any one in England. What a distinction! She might get into the first circles in London! She would want neither beauty nor fortune to recommend her! She would be a match for any man who had a taste for music.' While a correspondent, writing in 1800 in the *Allgemeine Musikalische Zeitung*, points out: 'Every well-bred girl, whether she has talent or not, must learn to play the piano or to sing: first of all, it's fashionable: secondly . . . it's the most convenient way for her to put herself forward attractively in society and thereby, if she's lucky, make an advantageous matrimonial alliance, particularly a moneyed one.'[1]

But whereas the nineteenth century may have been guilty of a naïve misplacement of values, in putting social status before personal satisfaction, the twentieth century makes the more fundamental error by stressing the competitive element. As Sigmund Mark points out:[2] 'Immediately the Self is being forced to pursue cultural learnings in order to reach impersonal and competitive standards, the process loses its cultural values, and becomes just another impersonal learning. Therein lies the danger that we are introducing into a process which is most personal in need, speed and evaluation, all the enemies of cultural development, such as tension, fear of failure and criticism, discouragement, conceit, and lack of faith in oneself.'

Music approached in this light becomes the means rather than the end. We must acknowledge that it does have many functions: as the handmaid of religion; as a therapeutic tool; as a social grace or a mere something 'while you work'. But we should all, through an active and full *participation* in music, aspire to that goal of all serious art-lovers where, as Percy C. Buck has well said,[3] 'critical

[1] Quoted by Arthur Loesser, *Men, Women and Pianos* (Gollancz, 1955), pp. 281 and 137–8.   [2] 'Personal Factors in Music Education', *The Music Teacher* (May 1952).
[3] *The Scope of Music* (O.U.P., 1924), p. 71.

appreciation makes life an inexhaustible well of joy. It is a road everyone can travel, and all of us do travel some distance along it. . . . Only a fool will ever think the end of the road has been reached, for there is no end, and only conceit will allow anyone to think he has gone as far as he might have gone. And the going a little further, which is possible to all of us, will not only result in an increase of our own enjoyment of life, but will also prevent that atrophy of our power of enjoyment which . . . may make our later years emotionless and grey.'

4

Why Play *the Piano?*

'He who does not love music is not yet human; he who loves it only is only half human; but he who loves and practises it—he is fully human.' (Goethe)

To re-affirm with Shelley that 'The soul's joy lies in doing' is very necessary in this technological age of material affluence and increased leisure time for the masses. But it is not only the *newly* leisured to whom the use of leisure time presents a recognized problem. Other sections in the community are exhibiting symptoms of leisure time maladjustment. For example, the greater part of two hundred housewives between the ages of 23 and 50+ who in May 1961 wrote to the *Observer*, in response to a series of articles entitled 'Miserable Married Women', claimed that they had experienced 'boredom, loneliness or guilt' (in some cases all three) at not doing 'something useful' with their leisure time. As I was, just then, being inundated daily with testimony to the beneficial effects of pianoforte playing as a leisure-time activity, I wrote to the editor to point this out, and added: 'The mother has always played an important rôle in promoting musical activity in the community by initiating and encouraging the efforts of her own children in this field.[1] She has not, however, always recognized its potential value to herself!'

The newspaper's subsequent article, which began with a quotation from my letter, indeed confirmed this: ' "They may not have considered the possibility of pianoforte playing" a well-meaning reader suggests. I have to admit that none of the 200 wives who wrote to us had. But many had thought of something, and stopped short of despair.'

[1] Mendelssohn in the past, and Shura Cherkassky today bear eminent witness to this claim.

Some members of the community, however, have not 'stopped short of despair'. In December 1961 the Chairman of the British Medical Association's Hobbies Exhibition referred to the increasing number of cases of mental illness and hypochondria attributable to the increase in leisure time, and urged doctors to 'prescribe hobbies rather than pills'.[1] And, significantly, it was only three years previously that the Society for Musical Therapy and Remedial Music[3] was set up in England with the object of 'promoting the use of music in the treatment, education, training and rehabilitation of children and adults suffering from emotional, physical or mental handicaps.'

There was a time when to participate actively in music-making was the accepted mark of a civilized man. Indeed, 'listening to music', as distinct from taking part in it, as Roger Sessions points out,[2] is a relatively late, a relatively sophisticated, and even a rather artificial means of access to it'. It might, he maintains, be reasoned that 'the listener has existed as such only for about 350 years. The composers of the Middle Ages and the Renaissance composed their music for church services and for secular occasions . . . or else they composed it for amateurs who had received musical training as a part of general education, and whose relationship with it was that of the performer responding to it through active participation in its production. Even well into the nineteenth century the musical public consisted largely of people whose primary contact with music was through playing or singing in the privacy of their own homes. For them concerts were in a certain sense occasional rituals which they attended as adepts, and they were the better equipped as listeners because of their experience in participating, however humbly and however inadequately, in the actual process of musical production.'

Further, a curious and unexpected analogy with our 'civilized man' is to be found in America where, since leisure time itself is a commonplace, the use to which it is put is now the criterion of social standing. There the popularity of 'spectator' sports and other types of passive recreation increases as one moves down the social

[1] From a report in *The Daily Telegraph*, 5 December 1961.

[2] *The Musical Experience of Composer, Performer, Listener* (Princeton University Press, 1950).

[3] Now called the British Society for Music Therapy.

scale. 'In contrast, members of the two upper classes show a marked preference for active, creative activities.'[1] Thus piano-playing, as an example of an active, creative hobby, should—provided England continues increasingly to reflect American type socio-economic patterns (as she has many indications of doing)—enjoy enhanced prestige here also. Indeed, here it has never lost its strong nineteenth-century middle-class associations. The persistence of this attitude was recently demonstrated at a conference by a teacher who claimed that if the 'profile' system was adopted in lieu of the existing 11+ selection system for secondary education it would be more 'pernicious' in that it would *pick out middle-class children with clean clothes who spoke nicely to the teachers, took piano lessons*, and so on'.[2] (My italics)

There is also the very special problem posed by the leisure of retirement. In his sane and stimulating book, *Man Against Aging*,[3] Dr Robert de Ropp asks why, in view of all the worthwhile activities in which a man may engage his powers of learning and understanding, 'do so many elderly people . . . permit themselves to rot in idleness?' He goes on: 'Here we face a very fundamental problem of ageing which for lack of a better term we call loss of motivation. . . . The motives which work splendidly in youth and middle age may, as old age approaches, lose their attractions. When this happens the ageing individual is apt to come to a standstill like a watch whose spring has run down.' And, unless he can find other 'challenges' to act as motivators to effort, he does, through this lack of adequate interests and activities, hasten his own decline.

Whatever choice of retirement hobby then is made to offset this lack of challenges to effort, it is important that, as Dr de Ropp stresses, 'the retirement occupation should bear some relationship to the pattern of a man's existing skills'.

Thus, though we may not yet have attained the age when retirement is imminent, we should be already well started on some active, creative part-time activity. The following chapter considers some of the indications for choosing the piano as our instrument, if we are musically inclined. And, as I shall suggest later (Chapter 11), there are very few persons indeed who are *not* musical!

[1] Vance Packard, *The Status Seekers* (Pelican Books, 1961), p. 135.
[2] From a report in *The Daily Telegraph*, 16 July 1964.   [3] Gollancz, 1961, p. 270.

5

Why play the Piano?

'I observed that hardly one lighter or boat in three that had
the goods of a house in, but there were a pair of Virginalls
in it.' (Samuel Pepys, on the Great Fire of London, 1666)

ALTHOUGH the piano has never lost its pre-eminence as the basic
educational instrument for the serious musician, let us now look at
some of the reasons that commend it to the amateur today.

I let the following adult beginners speak for themselves.

'Studying the piano has altered my life completely,' wrote a
48-year-old civil servant. 'It is now absolutely full and exciting.
Mysteriously I do much more "other work" since the piano started
than before—the garden looks good and the decorating gets done.
The result of the more you do the more you can. Not only that, but
piano-playing has taught me the value of patience and attention to
detail in other work.' His reasons for taking up the piano (at the age
of 42) were various, 'the chief one probably being a gap left in life by
death of eldest child; general dissatisfaction with passive forms of
entertainment, and a certain emptiness of the common round of
events, and a realization of having done nothing in particular except
live, influenced my decision to try to play the piano'.

While a 39-year-old housewife wrote: 'I am an extremely emotional person, and music can transport me into higher planes above.
I find that the study of music gives me the outlet I need. I can
pour my moods into my playing and come away refreshed and
rested.'

A 21-year-old secretary wrote: 'I most certainly do feel that the
study of the pianoforte at an adult age is worthwhile. It helps to keep
one's brain alert, and it gives endless hours of enjoyment to oneself
and often to many other people too. It is often a means of earning a
little extra money as well.'

A 31-year-old housewife commented: 'I have found it extremely worthwhile to be learning piano (A) because it has increased my enjoyment in listening to music, (B) I have learnt to read music, (C) I can help my children with their piano practice, (D) I have been able to satisfy an ambition I have had for many years—to make music myself instead of always being a listener.'

And a young man of 21 observed frankly that piano-playing is 'an asset in every way as it is a wonderful thing for being the centre of attention'. While the more mature view of a grandmother was given as follows: 'I feel any time I have been able to devote to the study of music has been most rewarding in every way. Not only to myself but all one comes in contact with I feel benefit.'

'Piano-playing is a never ending game of skill,' said Herbert Fryer, and it is a game that can be played solo, with a partner, or as a member of a team. The skill can be enjoyed at all levels: the beginner can make music on the piano more easily and completely than on any other instrument; and (provided the piano is tuned regularly) will perform 'in tune'—not like the beginner on a string instrument whose initially untrained ear must act the policeman to an erring finger in selecting its correct position on the string. And whilst the acquisition of additional technical skill can be an absorbing and never-ending challenge, even in the very early stages the budding pianist, partnered by a more skilled musician in the 'maestro e scholare' type of duet (in which one part is decidedly easier than the other), can enjoy a sense of achievement from the total musical effect he has himself helped to produce.

As more and more skill is acquired the resources of the instrument become increasingly apparent, until we reach the stage when the piano can be used as 'the domestic orchestra', as Sir Walford Davies used to call it. Today, when first-rate recordings of orchestral works are readily available, the piano transcription of an orchestral score is not made use of as widely as in the past. However, arrangements for solo piano of well-known pianoforte concertos[1] can give enormous enjoyment. One can go on to tackle the original score in the capacity of 'soloist', with an obliging teacher or musical friend working away as 'tutti' on a second instrument, until an opportunity arises for performing the work with an amateur

[1] See Appendix 2, Repertoire, Section 7, How to Win Friends.

orchestral group. (Mozart's Concertos K.414 and K.488, both in A major, are suitable ones to start with.)

Again, as 'the compleat accompanist' the piano has no near rival; while in lieder and in later instrumental sonatas the pianist, far from 'following discreetly', has an equal share in the performance. And he may also participate in varied chamber music ensembles.

However, if our amateur pianist is of a solitary mind, there is nothing to prevent him from locking himself away in his own ivory tower and making his personal selection of works for solo performance from the largest repertory that exists for any musical instrument! The pianoforte has taken over all the works written for its predecessors, the virginals, clavichord, and harpsichord. It proudly claims the great sonatas of the classical period, and revels in the poetical and emotional wealth of nineteenth-century Romanticism. It boasts of distinguished music by the nationalist schools of more modern times, including that of the exquisite French Impressionists, and shares in the complexities of contemporary idioms, with their exhilarating challenges. The piano, indeed, as a basically non-melodic instrument, would seem to be the ideal medium for performing 'pointillistic' works, with their apparently isolated, unrelated notes.

As regards public performances, the amateur pianist is in constant demand as choral accompanist, official pianist for the Women's Institute, to play at children's parties, for the minority religious group that does not boast an organ, and for various functions at the newer community centres. The local amateur dramatic operatic society will depend on him when putting on a 'musical' or a pantomime, and he will find himself vying with professionals in providing light entertainment in hotels and public houses. There is a place for him in the jazz group, or with a local dance band, and at the dancing school he will be found at the keyboard helping to mould the young dancers' sense of rhythm far more effectively than any impersonal record-player.

There is certainly a place for the amateur pianist in society today. His numbers are flourishing, and his services are in demand.

c

6

Never Too Late

'Music adds years to your life and life to your years.'
(Dr le Roy B. Campbell)

'Is it any use my going on, do you think?' a semi-retired school-master in his sixties asked me one day at the end of his piano lesson. 'I feel by the time I can do anything I shall be fading out!'

That same week I received my first 'case history' for this book. It came from a pianoforte teacher of 68 who had herself been an absolute beginner at 50! In fact, as C. M. Fleming has said:[1] 'It is never too late to learn; but learning is possible only if the would-be learner believes he can learn and is prepared to take the necessary steps.'

Psychological research into the ability to learn, though far from conclusive, has at least established that *the ability to learn declines far more slowly with advancing years than most people assume*. Careful psychological tests on persons motivated with the desire to learn indicate that the ability to learn at 80 is approximately the same as at 12, with the peak occurring around 22 years. Adults of 25–45 can be expected to learn at nearly the same rate as adolescents of age 15–20. But what that rate is will depend upon the general intelligence and special capacities of the individual; not upon his age-group. Further, the assumed decline in the ability to learn with increasing age can largely be offset by continual practice in learning.

However, an adult can inhibit his ability to learn by regarding himself as being unduly handicapped as compared with the child. Society, too, largely identifies the activity of learning with childhood and adolescence (though this is a social convention dependent on economic factors), and thus the adult assumes that this association

---

[1] *The Social Psychology of Education* (Kegan Paul, 1944).

is a fact of life. He tries to make up for this presumed drawback of his by adopting an over-anxious attitude towards piano-playing and this, in matters of technique especially, can create those very muscular tensions that often loom so large among his problems.

Where pianoforte teachers can be heard acknowledging the differences between the muscular difficulties experienced by children and adults, the problem most often reduces itself to the simple statement that the adult has 'stiff muscles'. Yet the great advance in the study and analysis of the physiological processes involved in pianistic technique that have occurred in this century largely meet this objection, as they enable the adult to produce far more accurately those movements and muscular states necessary to his technical development.

We are accustomed to witnessing the professional artist of mature years performing feats of technical virtuosity. We can rightly argue that he had the benefit of early training, and may very probably have commenced his career as a child prodigy. But we should not ignore the evident fact that the continual practice and performance in which he engages largely offsets any natural tendency to physiological degeneration. Casals, the famous cellist, is reported as saying, at the age of 70, that he practised searchingly every day, and found immense pleasure in seeing that he could still learn.

Practice, indeed, is a most valuable tool, both for advancing technique and for offsetting physiological degeneration, and as such should be grasped eagerly by every adult beginner. I shall discuss some of the measures for ensuring successful practice in Chapter 8.

A few years ago, when I had just begun thinking out the implications of the physiological aspects of late piano learning, and was ruminating on the difficulties experienced by adult beginners in co-ordinating the use of various muscles, I met a very charming lady who had just gained her civil air pilot's licence at the age of 60. Here, indeed, was an activity demanding quick decisions, and rapid muscular responses!

It certainly seems pertinent then to bear in mind that not only is it possible, in various fields, to achieve success in spite of a late start (Grandma Moses didn't *begin* painting her primitives until she was 78!) but that, although man's greatest creative achievements occur most often during the thirties, some of the world's most outstanding creative works have been produced in later middle life or old age. For example, Handel's *Messiah* was composed at the age of 56; Samuel Johnson finished writing the most famous of his books, *Lives of the English Poets*, at 72; the second part of Goethe's *Faust* was completed when he was 80; and Verdi's last work for the stage, *Falstaff*, regarded by many as his masterpiece, was first produced at Milan in 1893, his eightieth year.

'You see,' to quote Cicero in *De Senectute*, 'old age is so far from being feeble and inactive that it is ever industrious, always doing and devising something . . . ever learning something new. Solon, for example, boasts in his verses of learning something new every day. I too have done likewise in learning the Greek language in my old age. I grasped it greedily, as if I were desirous of satisfying a long protracted thirst. . . . And when I heard that Socrates had taken up the lyre as an old man, I decided I should like to do that too, for the ancients used to learn the lyre, and I have studied their literature.

'Nor even now do I feel the want of the strength of a young man . . . no more than when a young man I felt the want of the strength of a bull or of the elephant. *What one has, that one ought to use; and whatever you do, you should do it with all your strength.*'

7

How long will it take and how far can I get?

UNLIKE the man who, on being asked 'Can you play the piano?' replied, 'I don't know, I haven't tried!', the average adult beginner wants to know just how long it is going to take him to learn, and what standard of accomplishment he may confidently expect to attain in that time.

The short answer is that adult beginners can, and do, attain professional diplomas, such as the L.R.A.M. or A.R.C.M., but these achievements are exceptional in exactly the same way as they are for the pupil who begins to learn in childhood. But the time taken for the average adult beginner to reach any one standard of proficiency, while varying according to individual circumstances, should generally be less than that taken by the average child. There is, however, a tendency for very large numbers of would-be pianists of any age to cease to make further progress after reaching only a half-way standard of attainment.

Statistics published annually by the Associated Board of the Royal Schools of Music, probably the largest examining body in this country, demonstrate this general falling off in persistence as the technical and interpretative demands on candidates increase progressively through the grades, from I (Primary) to 8 (Final).

An examination of these statistics[1] over a 15-year period (1947–61) reveals that whereas approximately twenty thousand candidates annually attempt the First Grade examination, about fifteen hundred will take the Final (Eighth) Grade; while after the Middle Grades the falling off is quite dramatic, the number of entrants being reduced by roughly a half at each stage after Grade V.

Obviously not all piano pupils enter for examinations. However,

[1] These statistics refer to all age-groups. I am informed that separate figures relating to adult candidates only are not available.

an estimate based on graded educational music sold (cited in the *Music Teacher* of May 1962) further supports the view that the majority of piano pupils of any age group apparently stop learning when they reach a standard of proficiency approximating to the middle grades.

What kind of music, then, can be played by performers who have reached this 'half-way house'? The lists to be found on pages 75–76 give an indication. I have included pieces which not only have adult appeal, but whose idiom is readily acceptable to the average musical ear, ranging from examples of early keyboard works, through the Classical and Romantic styles, to works by some modern composers.

Incidentally, the adult beginner should not feel that because a piece is of moderate difficulty only he is wasting his time on 'kid's stuff'. Many of the Beethoven *Bagatelles*, for instance, are mature works. Indeed they form a treasury of miniatures for the pianist, and even the simpler ones listed here are frequently to be heard in professional recital programmes. Radio enthusiasts too will be familiar with Beethoven's 'Für Elise', beloved of B.B.C. producers of period plays; while Music Magazine's signature tune, Gerald Moore's arrangement of Schubert's 'To Music', is merely of Grade IV standard of difficulty.

For the adult who may object that Schumann's *Scenes of Childhood* and *Album for the Young* are not for him we have the composer's own statement to the effect that the former are 'reminiscences of an old person for old folk', whereas the pieces in the *Album for the Young* are 'rather foreshadowings, anticipations for young folk'. No less a pianist than Backhaus is reported as saying: 'Why seek difficulty when there is so much that is quite as beautiful and yet not difficult? Why try to make a bouquet of oak trees when the ground is covered with exquisite flowers?'

The adult beginner, then, may like to use these lists as a yardstick against which to measure his own present standard of achievement, or to make selections from them to extend his repertoire.

By choosing pieces from a graded list he will avoid the possible frustration of attempting an enticing work for which he is not yet equipped either technically or musically.

The less conservative adult beginner will of course, in addition, want to explore the lists of graded contemporary music also to be found in Appendix 2.

As regards the time involved in attaining this half-way standard, an experienced examiner has estimated that a child, commencing lessons at seven years of age would be likely to take Grade IV at twelve, and Grade V at about thirteen and a half. That is, the average examination child candidate (which we must take, in the main, to represent the more able child—the others having, presumably, fallen out en route) can be expected to take about six and a half years to attain Grade V (Higher). The average age for taking the eighth (Final) grade he estimated as nineteen: i.e. a total of twelve years training to pass through all the amateur grades.

How does this compare then with case histories of some of the more able adults supplied by their teachers in response to my questionnaires?

Teacher 1. 'My highest standard reached with an adult up to the present time is between grades IV and V (Associated Board). Time taken, about 4 years. Age at beginning lessons from scratch, 51.'

Teacher 2. 'Grade IV in about 3 years. Age at time of commencing lessons: late 30s.'

Teacher 3. 'Grade V (Associated Board). It took 4 years. The pupil began at 27.'

Teacher 4. 'I have had one success with a not quite beginner of 19 years. She did learn a little when small—but had forgotten most of it. We started by doing Grade II exam, then III, IV, V, and VI with the theory too. All of which she passed in about 3–4 years.'

Teacher 5. 'On occasion, adults have obtained the Advanced (i.e. Grade VII) stage of the Associated Board Exams after about 6 years' experience, beginning about 20 years of age.'

Teacher 6. 'I have had successful adult beginners studying up to Grade VIII Associated Board, others who have not stayed the course.'

Teacher 7. 'Grade VIII Associated Board. It took $3\frac{1}{2}$ years. Began lessons at 18 years of age after trying to teach herself. . . . I do not think she realizes how much talent she has.'

Teacher 8. 'I have had many cases of grown-up pupils who have done well and have reached at least the standard of Grade VIII (Final) of the Associated Board Examinations. In fact I can give the cases of at least 12 married women who have passed Grade VIII and some of my amateurs have even passed an L.R.A.M. to A.R.C.M. (Teacher's) just for the sense of achievement they desired!' She adds, 'But where the 30–40–50 year olds will gradually get there the *talented* (my italics) teenager will pass Grade VIII at 15 or 16 or even a Performer's Diploma at that age.'

Which brings us full circle in our conclusion that the specially gifted of any age will reach their goal swiftly; but the moderately gifted adult, as we have observed, can and often does proceed along the route more quickly than his junior counterpart.

Let us then consider some of the possible reasons for this.

In the first place the adult is learning because he has a definite desire to do so.[1] (A willingness to learn, as psychologists will remind us, is a necessary prerequisite of successful learning.) Many children, even in this twentieth century, are in the position of having been 'put to piano lessons' by a parent or someone in authority over them. Not all children are learning to play the piano because they have expressed an irrepressible desire to do so! Secondly, the intellectual capacity of the adult to surmount the difficulties encountered in trying to cope with musical notation for the first time is greatly superior to that of the young child who may still be struggling with reading his own language, and making his first attempts at simple mathematics. In addition, the adult, by virtue of his greater musical maturity gained over the years as an appreciative listener to many musical works and performances, brings a far more mature critical sense to his practice periods. A young child, on the other hand, until corrected at his weekly or bi-weekly lesson, will often quite happily produce extremely unmusical noises when left to his own devices in practice periods between lessons. While even the cost of lessons themselves may prevent an adult from wasting time either between or during lessons.

A further consideration in favour of the adult learner is that both the dimensions of the piano and the weight of the piano key are suited to the adult and not the child. The child pianist, unlike the violinist, is not able to practice during his early days on a half or three-quarter-size instrument, and change his instrument as his own body grows.

[1] Except, perhaps, in the case of some student teachers needing a modicum of skill to satisfy the requirements for Infant School teaching.

As regards the acquisition of technique, however, the child would appear to have the advantage, for he is able, given the correct guidance, to acquire this gradually and naturally over a long period. However it is not uncommon for a promising youngster, on reaching a musical college, to be told that he 'has no technique' and will have to be prepared to re-shape the technical habits he has acquired by assiduous practice over the years. It rather depends on whether his professor holds the same technical tenets as his former teacher. There are many wrong ways of playing the piano, but also quite a number of right ones!

Lastly, since there is no psychological reason why the mass of learning activities should be relegated to childhood; while, further, the best time to learn anything (and this too has been attested psychologically) is when we want to make use of the knowledge, it follows that if we do want to learn to play the piano now, then 'there is no time like the present'.

As clearly the adult need not set his sights at the half-way house of achievement only, he may now confidently aim at any musical targets up to Grade VIII. The lists on pages 76–79 constitute a small sample only of that great wealth of music waiting to be gathered into the treasure house of the amateur pianist's repertoire.

8

Technique of Practice

'There's a way to do it better—Find it!' (Thomas Edison)

'What constitutes your biggest problem?' the questionnaire asked, and back came the answer again and again: 'Lack of time for practising.'

Every busy person faces this problem. But Arnold Bennett, for instance, who combined a successful literary career with multifarious leisure-time activities such as sketching, yachting, walking and cycling, and playing billiards, was also a proficient amateur pianist—because he organized his various activities and made a space for each one. The busy housewife, however, may object that as soon as *she* succeeds in making a space some member of the family will suddenly make additional demands on her and fill it again! She must, of course, quietly but firmly insist on her claim to some small period in the twenty-four hours when she may express herself as an individual. And, having cleared her piano-playing space, she must safeguard it against further encroachments.

As amateurs we accept that our piano-playing time must be limited. But it should be a fairly simple matter (except in cases of undue domestic, professional, or business stress) to organize it with intelligence and determination. Indeed, it is the really busy person who seems always able, somehow, to squeeze in yet another activity. While even the harassed housewife, if she would but look at her work in the spirit of one conducting a 'time-and-motion' study for some other worker, will be amazed at the unnecessary labour she gives herself, wasting both time and energy thereby.

Our real task, therefore, having subjected working, travelling, and leisure hours to analytical scrutiny in order to conserve energy and economize on wasted time, is to seek to make the very best use we can of the practice time now available to us. The present chapter considers some of the means we may employ to this end.

But first let us briefly remind ourselves of the prerequisites for attaining success in any undertaking. Firstly, we must be quite clear in our mind and heart that this is what we want to do and not something else. Secondly, we must believe that the undertaking is a worthwhile one. Thirdly, we must remind ourselves that 'if a job is worth doing it is worth doing properly'. And lastly, we must be prepared to stick at it! Having satisfied ourselves on these points we will now consider:

WHEN, HOW, and WHAT to PRACTISE

Whatever time or times of the day have been selected for practice periods, one must not sit down to practise when feeling tired, either physically or mentally. Tired muscles, and inattention due to mental fatigue can only result in inaccuracies in reading, and in the innervating of wrong muscular processes; while further psychological fatigue will accrue from the lack of satisfaction caused by the resulting poor performance. And not only will the present effort remain unrewarding emotionally, but the following practice period will also be handicapped by the learned errors.

Attention to such things as adequate lighting and heating; the use of a slant-board or a bath for preliminary relaxation and refreshment when tired after a day's work; and the prior clearing up of any nagging duties that are likely to obtrude themselves on one's consciousness when trying to concentrate—all these should be considered as aids to practice.

The type of practice should vary according to circumstances. Many people, for instance, find the morning hours (even to the extent of rising an hour earlier before breakfast) the best time for working on technique. While the evening hours are often found to be best for interpretation. (At certain late hours the active critical faculties of the mind tend to dim, and a kind of inspirational or intuitive perception of interpretation can then take over. It is, however, wise to check such 'illumined' moments by using a tape recorder, and listening to the 'inspired performance' the next day. The achievement may only have appeared to be greater because of the depressed functioning of the critical faculty at the time.)

Many adult beginners, for obvious domestic and/or work reasons, may not be able easily to arrange to practise in the morning, and many persons assert that they do not really come alive until evening anyhow (due largely to their different metabolic rhythm). But educational psychologists seem to be agreed that for hard mental work the morning hours do produce the best results. Thus for studying new material, and for memorizing, as well as for working on technique, the morning—when muscle tone and mental acuity have been renewed after a good night's rest—would generally seem to be the best time.

In addition, practice periods should be so spaced as to enable frequency of repetition to forestall the rate of forgetting.[1] At the same time, however, new skills or material, of a similar nature to that newly learned, should not be attempted too soon, as 'interference' in the consolidation of the prior skill can be caused thereby. The inner process of maturation cannot be hastened but only retarded by such pressures.[2]

For most adult beginners then the rule for practising will be 'little and often', and preferably in the morning, though all such recommendations should be checked by personal experiment. The mere fact of making a regular habit of practising at particular times will endow such times with greater effectiveness as practising periods, since habit will reinforce the 'psychological set' to get off to a good start at these times.

In addition the mood of the moment should be taken into

---

[1] In this connection it is worthy of note that Grace Rubin Rabson, who has done extensive research on the memorizing of pianoforte music, concluded that 'distributed practice periods' are desirable for beginners, but that experienced players show no difference in memorizing ability between distributed and 'block practice'.

[2] 'Interference' was demonstrated a few years ago in a promising child pianist of mine whose piano work was set back over a period of about twelve months after she had been put to violin lessons. Her piano 4th finger came to be substituted for the 5th; and curiously, though bass clef reading became impaired, the treble clef reading in no wise improved. The child also marked time in her general musical maturation throughout this period—which, incidentally, was not co-incidental with any psychological 'plateau' of consolidation. The moment for the commencement of the violin lessons relevant to the child's existing musical progress (on which I had not been consulted) had been ill chosen.

Indeed an over-zealous parent can greatly impede a child's natural rate of musical maturation, most commonly by persuading a music teacher to force a pupil into the certificate-grabbing race.

account. If it is screaming out for emotional satisfaction, then one should sit down and play for all one's worth any pieces one feels like and happens to know, or, if one is a good sight-reader, pile up volumes of music of all kinds and give oneself a cathartic concert. At such times it would be quite wrong to say: 'This is the time of day allotted for my practice, ergo I will now work for note accuracy and technical skills.' No, we must reconcile the puritan and voluptuary within ourselves and, further to this end, we should have *a flexible scheme of work embracing different aspects of musical study which involve us at different levels.*[1]

We will thus have a number of pieces 'on the go'—preferably embracing different styles so as to include an early contrapuntal work, a classical sonata, a romantic piece, and a modern or contemporary work—all at various stages of preparation from the initial study of the score to the final stage of 'practice for performance', in which actual performing conditions are aped as nearly as possible.

We must also have a graded scheme of work in *aural training* and *keyboard harmony*. This should include such things as reproducing a heard melody: vocally, on the keyboard, and by writing it down; singing a melody from score; practising on the keyboard and recognizing by ear basic chord progressions; and working, at the keyboard, at modulation and transposition—doing all these, not necessarily to be able to improvise, but to create a true musicianly basis which will facilitate and add depth to the learning of our cherished pieces.

A fully annotated list of books of graded courses to assist in this aspect of our work will be found in Appendix 1 under the following sections: Cultivating the Ear, p. 64; Keyboard Harmony, p. 68, Melody Making, Modulation, and Transposition at the Keyboard, pp. 67–68; Practical Musicianship (General), p. 70.

Sight-reading (Prima Vista), i.e. performing from the copy at first sight, depends primarily on our powers of visual organization. It has to be practised as a separate skill. It does not follow, as many believe, that good memorizers are necessarily bad sight-readers and

---

[1] The professional writer does this sort of thing when, feeling himself not particularly productive of new ideas he will devote an hour or so to routine tasks such as sorting out press cuttings, or attending to necessary correspondence and other business matters.

vice versa. A highly developed skill in one or the other tends, sometimes, to make it appear unnecessary to work at the less developed skill. For example, an accompanist with good powers of sight-reading may, with some justification, feel that he does not need to practise memorizing his music in the sense of 'playing without the copy', since he is able to have his copy before him when performing. As a good sight-reader, he will however be employing quite respectable feats of short-term memory, since he will be reading music several bars ahead of the one he is actually playing. On the other hand, a young child who is blessed with an exceptionally 'good ear' and keyboard sense may 'have the music by heart' almost from a first slow playing through. Such a child, obviously, does not feel the necessity for working at sight-reading as her satisfaction is so immediate to her present need, i.e. to be able to play enjoyable pieces on the piano. Most of us, however, would be well advised to make use of both strings to our bow.[1]

Incidentally, many persons of my generation were forbidden to 'play without the music'. It was somehow sinful to 'have it by heart'. Reading the music, like justice, not only had to be done but, by the presence of the copy on the music desk during performance, had clearly to be seen to be done. While 'playing by ear' (i.e. without having *seen* a copy)—or, with slightly less acrobatic associations, 'ear playing' as it is now more often called, was decidedly 'not done'. It is not impossible that the difficulty in memorizing music experienced by very many adult beginners may be attributable to an unconscious feeling of guilt, since by attempting now to play without the copy they are 'rebelling' against the authoritative strictures implanted in early childhood.

Studies

In our general scheme of work we must allocate a time for technical drills,[2] and further we must resolve for ourselves the question of how much our Czerny is really necessary! To practise studies constantly because a daily dose has been prescribed may satisfy our conscience but will not promote our musical welfare

---

[1] Recommended books on Memorizing and on Sight-reading will be found on pages 65 to 67 of Appendix 1.

[2] See Appendix 1, p. 71, for recommended books on Technical Exercises.

unless such studies have been selected with reference to our specific needs.
And indeed it is often more economical, in terms of time expendi-
ture and profit, to use a drill based on material abstracted from the
piece in which a technical difficulty manifests itself. For instance one
can practise the difficult passage with the most difficult fingering
possible (whereby a return to the original fingering will then seem
to be so much easier); practise the passage with the same fingering
throughout all keys,[1] no matter how awkward it may then become;
play the passage with different rhythmic accentuations; play the
passage on the key surfaces without depressing the keys; and even
rehearse the performance of the difficult passage mentally. There
also tends to be, Frank Merrick claims, 'the difficult pace' for any
given passage, which may vary from player to player. 'What is
here recommended,' he writes,[2] 'is that in long, swift successions of
single notes, such as in many Bach movements or Czerny Studies,
we should find out the pace at which the notes are the most tottery
and then assiduously play long stretches through at that exact pace.
In a few days the difficulty and staggerings will gradually melt out
of existence. . . . It is not often,' he rightly comments, 'that playing
something badly with conscious realization of the fact proves
positively beneficial.'[3]

Further, as Professor Lowery reminds us,[4] 'Transfer of learning
only takes place between subjects that have common factors. It is
useless therefore to expect any appreciable transfer between the
stock piano studies that deal only with the mechanical elements of
scales, broken chords and arpeggios on the one hand and the complexities of modern music on the other.' Of course, one must add,
educational studies did not cease with Czerny, Clementi, Cramer
& Co.: Béla Bartók in his *Mikrokosmos* (six volumes, Boosey &
Hawkes) has provided us with his own graded introduction to his
pianoforte music. It is mainly a matter of recognizing the purpose

---

[1] For self-help books on Transposition, see Appendix 1, p. 68.

[2] *Practising the Piano* (Rockliff, 1958), p. 92 (see Appendix 1, p. 61.

[3] This would appear to constitute one of the very few instances of successfully
applying the 'negative practice' technique of associationist psychologists: a procedure
developed by Dunlap in connection with the elimination of errors in typing. By this
method the wrong response to a situation is practised but always with a 'set' or strong
desire to eliminate the incorrect response. (See also footnote 2 on page 41.)

[4] *The Background of Music* (Hutchinson, 1962), p. 160.

for which a particular study has been written (often given as a title) and selecting according to our needs. By viewing studies in this light we can cheerfully avoid much dull material, and gain more time in which to savour the delights of, say, a Chopin Etude where, incidentally, no one would care to suggest that such 'sugaring of the pill' had in any way detracted from its technical effectiveness. Indeed, the study that demands musical insight as a sine qua non of its performance is of the highest value, as one cannot then so easily lose oneself in the arid wastes of mechanical technical practice.

Muscular Exercises

Gone are the days when several hours on end devoted to a daily dose of finger exercises and scales and arpeggios in every possible fiendish permutation—often with a copy of the current romantic novel surreptitiously propped up on the music desk to relieve the monotony!—were considered advisable for young ladies and gentlemen of amateur aspirations. Sheer muscular drilling can, and should, be done *away from the keyboard* as much as possible so that there will be no danger of dulling either the ear or musical sensitivity. This can be regarded as a legitimate short cut to the acquisition of technique (Liszt, and even the harpsichordist Couperin, had recourse to such exercises), and will prove a very present help in technical trouble for the late-learner to acquire co-ordination and independence of muscular response, and for the re-starter, as a short cut to reconditioning his muscular responses to essentially pianistic requirements.

Further, such exercises have a general liberating effect on all our bodily movements. Indeed the reciprocal relationship that exists between normal postural habits and pianistic movements should be more widely recognized. As Professor Gát notes: 'Sitting or walking with a stiff body, incorrect breathing habits, rigid neck posture, etcetera, may spoil piano playing as much as the innervation of wrong technical solutions.'[1]

For adult beginners wishing to pursue this subject some recommended books will be found in Appendix 1, p. 71, as well as albums of exercises to be performed at the keyboard—when the most careful listening should always be brought to bear.

[1] *The Technique of Piano Playing* (see Appendix 1, p. 71.)

Scales and Arpeggios

Scales and arpeggios were, with two exceptions only, voted the most unpopular item in the amateur pianist's curriculum. This, like a fear of the dark, is the sort of attitude we adopt from others without questioning. Scales can be immensely fascinating—especially if one thinks in terms of, say, a harpsichord effect, a pearly Mozartian run, a dramatic Beethoven ascent, or a Debussyish veiled vagueness; if one soars up in a minor mode and returns joyfully, without a break, by way of its relative major, adjusting the compass at the extremes to allow for a convincing return and satisfying final tonic; if the two hands are set into lively competition and partnership by each performing in a different rhythmic grouping to the common pulse (such as one note against two, two against three, three against four, and so on); or with a different volume level (right hand accompanying left hand and vice versa); or by combining two different kinds of touch (legato R.H. with staccato L.H. and vice versa). It is all a matter of why we are practising them, of what we expect them to do for us. They are often regarded as a prime means for exercising and strengthening the fingers, but one has only to tot up the number of times the notoriously weak fourth and fifth fingers are used in a four-octave scale to realize the absurdity of this notion.

A. E. F. Dickinson observes:[1] 'Scales and arpeggios select the patterns of pitch-relationship which may most commonly be encountered *in one hand or the other* in a given key. They do no more. Scales and arpeggios in both hands are not common, and it is ridiculous to spend much time in extending the process, in preparation for innumerable imaginary contingencies, to every conceivable major and minor formula for each hand, especially the harmonic minors. Simple chordal sequences[2] in the common keys . . . are equally necessary and indeed more urgent material for dealing with the key-problem.' He continues: 'The same argument applies to scales and arpeggios treated as technical ground. They are limited in usefulness. *For such thoroughness the amateur has little time or need.*' (My italics)

[1] In an article on teaching the piano in *Musical Education* (Hinrichsen, 1945), p. 235.

[2] For recommended books on Keyboard Harmony see Appendix 1, p. 68.

D

As music teaching methods in this country are largely related to professional needs, it is not easy to assess just how much scale and arpeggio practice should be recommended for the amateur. I would point out, however, that all pianists, whether professional or amateur, are, in a sense, keyboard athletes, and as such should go into training. Apropos this I once heard Mr Sidney Harrison remark to a group of piano students that though he himself tended to resist scale and arpeggio practice he nevertheless recommended 'periodic bouts of masochistic self-torture' to aspiring pianistic technicians! Further, as L. P. Jacks has emphasized,[1] 'the human body is naturally *skill-hungry*, and until that hunger is satisfied it will be ill at ease, craving for something it has not got and seeking its satisfactions in external excitements which exhaust its vitality and diminish its capacity for joy'.

SECTION II: PIECES AT LAST!

'Think ten times and play once.' (Ferenc Liszt)

Memory

Clara Schumann, we are told, was castigated in her day because she dared to play her programmes from memory. Certain critics raised their eyebrows when Dame Myra Hess chose to play a concerto with the copy before her. Popular fashions tend to establish traditions. For instance, the soloists in an oratorio may sing with dignity and acclaim from behind their scores (to the relief of conductors, who cannot signal a whole orchestra to leap and catch an erring singer as will an experienced pianist accompanist), but woe betide the lieder singer who would dare to break the 'psychic link' with his audience by interposing *his* music. We must look again at this question of memorizing—especially, as many claim a piece is not really known until it *can* be played from memory.

Many psychologists believe memory, in its widest sense, to be the most important single factor necessary to our development as musicians. As music exists only in time, and not in space, without memory it would be meaningless to the listener, and, of course, impossible to perform even with a copy!

Of the three main factors in memory: (1) initial learning, (2) re-

[1] *The Education of the Whole Man* (University of London Press, 1931), p. 166.

tention, and (3) recognition and recall, only the first seems to be directly amenable to training. So we must look to our methods of learning if we wish to effect an improvement.

In spite of the claims of Gestalt psychologists, we must not suppose that it is necessarily a good thing to 'run through' a piece to 'see how it goes'. For that running through tends to get repeated and repeated until a kind of pseudo-practising evolves in which the pianist re-sight-reads the piece at each sitting. This method ensures the inclusion of all initial undetected errors, plus many more that may accrue at later stages. In the interests of simple note accuracy errors should not be allowed to occur, as they are not always easy to eradicate. Indeed, they have an unpleasant habit of making a sudden and unexpected return at a later date and at the least propitious moment! Further, as no detailed insight into the music has been sought, no standard of comparison for improving its performance is available—unless, of course, the adult beginner is resorting to a mere childlike imitation of someone else's performance of the work in question.

For any new piece two initial analyses are necessary: (A) musical, and (B) technical.

Musical Analysis

First of all the score must be studied overall in great detail and in a penetrating and imaginative frame of mind. The attitude of the loved one approaching her billet doux comes nearest to it. Professor Adler in *How to Read a Book*[1] describes it thus: people 'when they are in love and are reading a love letter, read for all they are worth. They read every word; they read between the lines and in the margins; they read the whole in terms of the parts, and each part in terms of the whole; they grow sensitive to context and ambiguity, to insinuation and implication; they perceive the colour of the words, the odour of phrases and the weight of sentences.'

Thus faced with the music for the first time, one must first note such things as the title, composer, and period of the work, its mood(s) and likely tempi, key(s) and modulatory material, changes of texture and overall shape. Then one must scrutinize the hints

[1] Pub. Jarrolds. I am indebted for this delightful analogy to an unsigned article, 'The Reading of Music', in the *Music Teacher* of April 1948.

towards its interpretation given by the editor and/or composer. Ritenuto, stringendo, sforzando and pianissimo, staccato, legato, slur and mezzo-staccato, tenuto, accelerando, diminuendo and da capo, are all there with a purpose. If we slavishly reproduce them without integrating that purpose with our own musical conception and intention, we are but sham performers, a species of non-recreative copyists.

After this preliminary scrutiny the work can be played straight through at a comfortable pace so that the ear can learn its sounds. Some people may be able to hear mentally the principal melodies and underlying harmony, and will need to teach their ear only one or two less familiar pitch combinations. While others, who have not yet advanced their faculty for visual/aural association, will have to try to retain aurally/mentally as much as possible from one or two careful playings-through.

The work can then be 'conducted' away from the keyboard, the imagination being brought to bear on such things as tempi, colour and quality of tone, dynamic range, phrase shape and rhythmic progression (as an American friend of mine remarked: 'Music's always going someplace'). The work can also be sung either vocally, where possible, or mentally, and at a later stage a mental/aural rehearsal without the score will serve to reinforce the musical memory as well as help to develop musical insight.

Also, the practice of singing the music *when performing* is of particular value to the pianist, who is not dealing with a primarily melodic instrument. That renowned teacher, Leschetizky (1830–1915) is reported as saying: 'If you can tell when someone is playing that he is singing the music in his mind as he plays it, it is a good performance, and if you cannot, it is a bad performance.'

Further, if we are conscientious in our desire to develop our interpretative powers, we should defer seeking to listen to a live or recorded performance of a work until we have exhausted all our own ideas. Then we can make an intelligent comparison of our own musical conception with that of, preferably, several artists, and seek to discover not only where their performances differ from each other and from our version but also the musical reason for those differences. I believe it is a mistake for an adult to say to his teacher: 'Will you play this piece over for me to see how it goes?' A child may gradually assimilate a feeling for interpretation by imitating his teacher, supplemented, one hopes, by a certain amount of analytical work and opportunity for bringing his own ideas and feelings to a performance, but the adult already has much past musical listening experience behind him on which to draw for guidance. His task is one of analysing that experience and bringing it to bear on the work in hand. His teacher's task, in this context, is to assist him towards the right technical solutions to express his musical concept, and to guide the latter by an appeal to period style and basic musical logic (i.e. the harmonic/melodic and 'formal' language of music) when these are erring.[1]

Technical Analysis

In this section on learning pieces I have purposely placed the consideration of musical interpretation before that of technical analysis, and would emphasize that there is absolutely no case for 'practising the notes first and putting in the expression afterwards'. Unless the pianist knows the kind of sound he wishes to produce— whether brilliant or cantabile, persuasive or firmly authoritative, delicate or roundly resonant—he cannot decide what type of touch to employ in his practice. Further, if he does not have an approximately correct conception of the performance speed of the piece he may. in certain passages, be employing technical movements which are suited to slow playing but not to fast. He then has either to learn a new set of technical movements for the piece at speed or to remain insufficiently agile because of having innervated by practice the wrong technical movements.

I think Busoni may have had something like this in mind when in a letter[2] to his wife he wrote, regarding the rules for practising the piano: 'Don't set your mind on overcoming the difficulties in pieces which have been unsuccessful because you have previously practised them badly; it is generally a useless task. But if meanwhile *you have quite changed your way of playing*, then begin the study of the old piece from the beginning as if you did not know it.' (My italics)

---

[1] Books on Style and Interpretation, Musical Form, Melody Making, Modulation, Harmony, Improvization, and Musicianship are listed in Appendix I, pp. 61–64, 67–70.

[2] *The Essence of Music* (Rockliff, 1957), p. 81.

I have not wished to imply that slow practice should never be undertaken. It can be used with advantage for specific purposes; for example, to allow a slow ear to detect irregularities in a florid passage where the fingers had 'taken over' before the mind had a clear conception of it at speed; to imprint a particular fingering on the memory (here staccato practice can also help); to obtain accuracy and confidence in easier pieces whose ultimate performing speed does not involve the special techniques of high-speed playing. Hence the oft-repeated injunction to children to practise slowly. The adult beginner likewise can make a gradual increase in his speed for such pieces by stepping up the metronome notch by notch. A word of warning is necessary here though. He must not expect to commence a subsequent practice period at the fastest speed he achieved at the end of his previous practice. He will find it advisable to move back a few notches to set himself off again, so as to allow for the slight loss on recently gained skill before it is finally consolidated by sufficient repetition.

The solution for reconciling initial care in preparation with final speed in performance, and one which to a certain extent combines the principles of both holistic (Gestalt) and piecemeal (contiguous conditioning) psychological views, lies in the use of what Frank Merrick[1] has aptly termed '*Delayed Continuity*', and which he owes to his former teacher, Leschetizky. In this method a phrase or melodic unit is mentally or actually sung at the correct performing speed. It is then played up to speed in imitation of the mental concept, and this playing is followed by a pause in which an assessment is made of the phrase performed, and such questions asked as—did the pedalling and fingering I used produce the result in sound that I intended? Now—and this is where the method calls for much self-control—the phrase must not be repeated after discovering what its faults were until it has once more been modelled mentally/aurally. Eventually the piece is built up phrase by phrase with the requisite pause for judgement and planning between each one, when the fingers remain in contact with the keys just released.

Mr Merrick comments of this method: 'When the pauses are long and profitably given up to effective planning and the tempo very

[1] *Practising the Piano* (Rockliff, 1958), Chapter 1. Annotated in Appendix 1, p. 61.

quick in the actual playing, we combine the muscular development and high spirits of speed with the safety and confidence of slow practice in a way that tends to eliminate a great deal of profitless drudgery. Some slow practice is unavoidable, but should it be often supplemented and sometimes superseded by this "look before you leap" kind of quick practice.'

If, however, your type of temperament cannot accept such discipline as this method entails, James Ching's solution to this problem may be useful to you. 'I have . . . found it possible,' he writes,[1] 'during the preliminary stage of slow practice, to *imagine* the different physiological conditions which have to be brought into operation when playing takes place at faster speeds. I believe that the ability thus to imagine, in the initial stage of learning, the correct and ultimate bodily sensation is of the greatest possible value in the prevention of the "wrong" habit from becoming "set" in the early stages.'[2]

Incidentally, fingering, which will vary according to the general method of technique employed, and the individual shape and size of the pianist's hand, is also affected by the speed of playing. The number of satisfactory fingering alternatives available for high speeds must obviously be less than for low ones. (Someone once observed that almost any feat is possible on the piano provided one had the time in which to execute it!)

In the mechanistic methods of the past interpretation has tended to limp after technique—nay, often to be crippled by it. Possibly by first seeking to develop the processes of musical maturation, technique itself will be developed far more easily because it will then be musically more goal-directed. We may even see, in the future, the adoption of sleep-state methods of learning, when the memorizing of an extensive repertoire with its presumed increase in musical perception would be possible in a fraction of the time required by normal methods.

In this short book there has been room for only a passing glance at some of the many aspects of piano study relevant to good practice, and it has been well nigh impossible to avoid controversy. If I have

[1] *Piano Playing: A Practical Method* (Bosworth, 1946), p. 317.
[2] This would furnish a further example of 'Negative Practice'. (See footnote 3 on page 33.)

succeeded in making the adult beginner take a new look at his own methods, and encouraged him to make further explorations in this most essential and rewarding field, I shall be content.[1]

[1] See Appendix 1 for books written especially for the Amateur Pianist, page 59; Self-help records for would-be pianists, page 58; Two books for accompanists, page 60; On Practising, page 61; Nervousness, page 61; Piano Technique, page 70; The Use of the Pedals, page 72; Two important books for pianists, page 72; Music—General Knowledge, page 73.

9

Have I got 'Pianist's Hands'?

NATURE, in her wisdom, did not see fit to provide us with two joints to our thumbs, or to make them and the 'little' fingers the same length as the remaining digits of the hand. Nor have piano manufacturers, for all their ingenuity, brought into general use a keyboard ideally adapted to the human hand. The length of the key is too short to permit full use of the stretched position most service-able for octave technique; and ideally the keyboard should be some-what semicircular rather than straight so as to offset the lack of control that arises from the extended position of the arms when playing at its extremes.

The notorious weakness of the 4th (ring) finger (probably due to the cross ligaments on either side of its tendons which serve to support the metacarpal bones of the hand) worried no less a person than Chopin, who in the last year of his life wrote apropos of technique: 'Nothing has come from my efforts except my long nose and my badly cultivated fourth finger.' Owing, incidentally, to its rather special construction, the 4th finger should never be exercised with both adjacent fingers held down—a common requirement of some of the older schools of finger exercises!

A restricted span between the fingers caused Schumann to exer-cise secretly with a home-made finger-adjuster. The result was a dislocated third finger, and the cessation of an intended career as a concert pianist. While Hamilton Harty, we are told, confessed to thirty years' efforts at training an unruly thumb afflicted by 'double joints'—Nature's supreme practical joke on intending pianists!

In spite of such examples, the romantic conception of the mys-tique of the 'pianist's hand' has somehow prevailed. 'Oh, listen to that scale which flows so sweetly,' a critic wrote of the young Gottschalk's playing in 1845. 'It is not the hand of a man that touches the keys, it is the wing of a sylph that caresses them.' And in 1873 a young American lady, who had travelled to Weimar in the hope of taking lessons from the great Liszt, described her first impressions of him: 'Liszt is the most interesting and striking looking man imaginable—tall and slight, with deep-set eyes, shaggy eye-brows, and long iron-grey hair, which he wears parted in the middle. His mouth turns up in the corners which gives him a most crafty and Mephistophelian expression when he smiles, and his whole appearance and manner have a sort of Jesuitical elegance and ease. His hands are very narrow, with long and slender fingers that look as if they had twice as many joints as other people's! They are so flexible and supple that it makes you nervous to look at them.'

Oh those long slender hands! Novelists, playrights, and film and television script-writers have so perpetuated the tradition that possessors of squat podgy hands must have felt more outplaced than young ladies with the wrong 'vital statistics'.

But the truth of the matter is, as Jozsef Gát establishes in his monumental work, *The Technique of Piano Playing* (Corvina, Budapest), *the shorter the fingers* (other than the thumb) *compared with the back of the hand the more they are suited to the development of velocity*. Indeed many famous piano hands are thick and heavy with a large fist and short fingers. Gát gives the physiological explanation as follows:[1] 'The interosseous muscles are situated near the fingers, their importance consequently manifests itself notably in fast playing, in rapid finger-technique. Their development is a precondition of finger-velocity. For this reason the proportion between the length of the fingers and the length of the back of the hand is—to a certain extent—an indication of the ability to acquire velocity. The shorter the fingers in proportion to the back of the hand, the better they are able to execute quick movements.

'The interosseous muscles function most easily in connection with a somewhat stretched finger-position because then the slightest contraction of the muscles results in flexion. . . . In the case of long fingers we are compelled to apply either a bent hand-position or— if we use the stretched position—a steep position of the back of the hand. In this position the finger-stroke starts from a considerably bent position, which means a diminution of its efficacy.

[1] Pp. 21–26.

'A disadvantageous ratio between the fingers and the back of the hand may be compensated—to a certain measure—by the relative length of the thumb. If the thumb is long, the fingers need be less bent, so that the back of the hand can assume a less steep position.' Incidentally, a scrutiny of the Lisztian hand, of which a plaster cast exists, reveals just this long compensatory thumb.

It is interesting to note that this connection between velocity and the stretched finger position is exploited by the Romantic School in its preference for the remoter tonalities which make more use of the black keys. As Gát notes, Chopin, for instance, evinces a preference for D flat and A flat major (stretched position), and hardly ever uses D major (bent position).

While in Chopin, again, we see an echo of his recalcitrant 4th finger put to good effect by the choice of fingering employed: 'The essential weakness of the human hand is turned to beautiful account,' notes Grove, 'for his passages are often devised in such a manner that the weak finger of the hands has to play the note which is to be comparatively unimportant.'

Apart from the weakness of the 4th finger—which is often inadvertently encouraged by substituting the use of the 3rd, especially in some chord playing, when the 4th is rightly called for—its length, relative to the 3rd and 2nd fingers, is important in the execution of trills. If the fingers employed in trilling are of similar length, one finger does not have to bend unduly to compensate, and it is thus easier to equalize their striking power. 'Finger equalization', incidentally, was the sine qua non of the early 'Viennese School' of piano playing (Hummel, 1778–1837, Czerny, 1791–1857, and Moscheles, 1794–1870 were its brilliant exponents), whose aim was 'equality and purity of tone, delicacy of nuance, lightness and speed'.

Whatever our attitude may be to palmistry it is at least interesting to note that to the chirologist, Mir Bashir, for example, a long 3rd (i.e. pianist's 4th) and 'little finger' (5th), which would, of course, tend to equalize their length with that of the 3rd and 2nd fingers, connotes, in the case of the 4th, 'love of the beautiful', while the little finger is 'associated with that aspect of the personality which deals with expression. . . . When this finger is long and well shaped, love of expression is innate'!

To continue itemizing our perfect pianist's hand: the longer the first phalange (i.e. that part of the finger next to the hand knuckle) is compared with the second, and third (finger-tip to top joint section), the more favourable is the proportion of the phalanges. Where the first phalange is short a tendency to strike not from the knuckle joint as is correct but from the finger joint between the knuckle and middle phalange will occur. This means that the vertical descent of the topmost phalange into the key, which should be encouraged in the earliest training, is impossible.

A massive finger is to be preferred to a slender one as regards beauty of tone as well as velocity. To quote Gát once more: 'The weight-effect comes much more easily to players with short massive arms. A short finger transmits the force of the muscles more fully than does a long thin finger, and thus greater resonance will be achieved.' For those of other proportions, however, we may note that: 'Teaching . . . serves to compensate defective endowments. The fingers can be taught to transmit—with the aid of the finger-ends—the impulse given by the first joint and pass on to the keys the weight-effect given by the arm.'

I once knew a wind-player, however, who was unable to take up the piano because his fingers were too fat!

In contrast, a lady I knew had such small hands that in her youth she had been employed as a Hollywood extra: at least her hands and feet were so employed, as these members were regularly filmed as substitute 'close-ups' for the 'star' whose own anatomy had not been so blessed. Her extended span would have fallen somewhat short of a sixth.

Another small-handed lady, an adult pupil in her fifties, experienced trouble with her right hand. This she was able to extend to the octave only with discomfort, and it was not possible for her to play any intervening notes simultaneously within the octave span. As her left hand was less restricted, for some time I attributed the right hand constriction to her occupation, that of dressmaker, but as gentle palmar massage and selected hand gymnastic exercises[1] effected no improvement, I suggested that some forgotten injury might be responsible. The lady then recalled such an injury, and was able to show me the faint operation mark that remained. And

[1] See Appendix 1, p. 71.

we contented ourselves thenceforward with selecting music from my 'small hands' repertory lists, and by making minor adjustments to the copy if she felt she could not bear to forego a particular favourite. My own hands, incidentally, which had always been small, actually grew noticeably larger when I took up the piano again after the age of twenty-one.

Few people listening to Harriet Cohen playing would guess that this very gifted pianist was the possessor of small hands! No, whatever our difficulties in this respect we should not be deterred from playing the piano if playing the piano is what we want to do. Cyril Smith did not stop playing when he lost the use of an arm through a stroke; while Paul Wittgenstein, who possessed only one arm, was able to inspire four major works for piano by various composers, including Ravel's Piano Concerto in D Major for the Left Hand.

The truth of the matter is that the pianist is a resourceful and adaptable creature. He has been abjured at one time or another to play his instrument by all manner of means. He has been instructed not to use his thumbs (a hangover from clavichord and harpsichord technique). Bach saw through that fallacy. He has been forced to practise with his arms stuck through an instrument somewhat resembling the pillory, and with each finger projecting through perforated brass plates called 'Finger Guides' (Logier's 'Chiroplast', patented 1814). He has tensed his muscles into a state of 'Pianists' Cramp', until rescued by the Relaxationists who, in their turn, especially through the misinterpretation of Matthay's teachings, have been responsible for a certain amount of pianistic impotence.

Liszt's approach to the keyboard was described by the music critic, Saphir, in the following terms: He 'is an amiable fiend who treats his mistress—the piano—now tenderly, now tyrannically, devours her with kisses, lacerates her with lustful bites, embraces her, caresses her, sulks with her, scolds her, rebukes her, grabs her by the hair, clasps her, then all the more delicately, more affectionately, more passionately, more flamingly, more meltingly; exults with her to the heavens, soars with her through all the skies and finally settles down with her in a vale of flowers covered by a canopy of stars.'

I may be here taken to task for 'high-lighting' the emotional aspect of performance, for deserting the purely physiological aspect. But music has its own inherent gesture which, translated into the ballet of our technical movements, creates a symbiotic relationship of musical meaning, emotional expressiveness, and atunement with the instrument. In considering technique we should never lose sight of the fact that the music's the thing. At a party, an ardent lady amateur pianist, excited at meeting both Josef Hoffman and Godowsky, exclaimed on shaking hands: 'What small hands you have, Dr Hoffman! And yours too, Mr Godowsky! How in the world, gentlemen, can you great artists play the piano so magnificently with such small hands?' Godowsky is said to have replied: 'Where in the world, Madam, did you get the idea that we play the piano with our hands?'[1]

[1] Charles Cooke, *Playing the Piano for Pleasure* (Simon & Schuster, 1960), p. 17.

Have I got a 'Musical Ear'?

'How sweet the moonlight sleeps upon this bank! Here we
will sit, and let the sounds of music Creep in our ears . . .'
(*The Merchant of Venice*, v. I. 54)

SCIENTIFICALLY SPEAKING, the sounds of music do not creep in our
ears, *vibrations* impinge upon the human ear and are translated into
musical sounds by the brain. But, although the workings of this inner
connection between the physiological and psychical processes has
not yet been satisfactorily explained, we can rejoice in the highly
stimulating realization that the perception of musical sound is
primarily subjective, and that it can be developed through training.

A 'musical ear' in the sense of a specially constructed physical
organ is, according to most authorities, a misconception. Against
Mozart's highly sensitive powers of hearing (attributed by some to
the abnormally wide hollow of his ear) we may compare the fact
that Robert Franz, the sensitive Lieder composer of the nineteenth
century, 'never enjoyed especially acute hearing' in a physical sense.
Beethoven too composed the late quartets from the wealth of his
phenomenal 'chant intérieur' when the physical organ of hearing no
longer functioned.

Nor is the possession of 'absolute pitch', or 'perfect pitch', i.e.
the ability to recognize an isolated sound as being a particular note,
such as Middle C, or to reproduce it vocally from score, an indication of the existence of a 'musical ear'. This ability, which is most
often associated with the middle three octaves of the piano—corres-
ponding roughly with the choral compass of voices—is not an un-
mixed blessing for a musician. For instance, I have known 'perfect
pitch' choristers forced into an embarrassed silence when the choir-

master has signalled his accompanist to transpose up a semitone; from that moment onwards every note was, for them, out of tune!

Complete absolute pitch is, however, somewhat rare, for in many cases those claiming to possess absolute pitch are using a combination of a limited ability in this field with the more common 'relative pitch', which is developed by the usual methods of aural training. 'Relative pitch', indeed, is of more importance to the musician than absolute pitch, and of particular interest to us since it is not merely an inherent gift, but is readily amenable to training.

Ear-training must indeed be undertaken by anyone who is engaged in the performance of music, not only as a means for self-criticism but also as a means for developing his musical perception. 'At a concert,' wrote Busoni, 'no one listens to me more attentively than I do myself. My mind is fixed on hearing and judging every note; indeed, my attention is so concentrated that I am incapable of thinking of anything else. I try to give the most faithful interpretation along with my own personal conception of the work I am playing. I am continually discovering new beauties, and *sometimes there flash upon me details of interpretation of which I had never dreamt before.*' (My italics)

Busoni had been complaining about pupils, and even many artists, who played mechanically. And it is, indeed, one of the pitfalls of piano learning that it is quite possible to play the piano without really listening! An amusing instance was reported of a child who went to tea at a friend's house where the little hostess duly performed on the piano. 'That's a nice piece,' said the guest, 'I would like to learn it. What is it called?' She then discovered, on looking at the copy, that it was the self-same piece she herself had proffered at a recent examination!

Apart from seeking to perfect his visual-aural perception for pitch, every performer should endeavour mentally to pre-hear, and then critically check, each sound he produces, both as to quality and intensity. This is not easy at the extremes of the piano's keyboard which covers seven to seven and a quarter octaves of the normal human ear's total of ten octaves of audibility—the biggest range for any single musical instrument, only excluding the organ.

String players often regard themselves as being greatly superior to pianists in aural ability. But pianists need to develop a special 'piano ear'. They must, by careful and constant listening, develop a sensitiveness to the possibilities of colour and dynamic range appropriate to the instrument, and be constantly on guard for the characteristically evanescent piano tone when trying to achieve a 'cantabile' effect. The piano, in its heyday, was called upon to do the very thing for which it seemed least fitted—i.e. to sing. For example, both Chopin and Mendelssohn exploit this attribute fully. Often, indeed, the mark of an amateur is a badly drawn melodic line, lacking in carrying quality and in tone-matching between adjacent notes, frequently accompanied by a misuse of rubato. If a single melodic line cannot be drawn clearly, then part-playing degenerates into a battle for the assertion of each 'entry'.

Again, if the pianist is unable to hear the identities of the separate factors in the chord, no amount of harmonic text book learning will enable him, say, to bring out the tonic in a six-four chord, or reduce the amount of tone he gives to the seventh in a dominant seventh. The ear, not the hand, is the arbiter in such niceties. And what of the melody plus accompaniment performed by one hand (such as in Mendelssohn's *Lieder Ohne Worte*, Op. 38, No. 2 in C minor)? Without a trained 'aural director' to take charge, such writing becomes a meaningless jangle on performance.

The arhythmic ear, i.e. one defective in the sense of time,[1] fails to detect the minute irregularities in timing and touch of shorter value notes. In florid passages this can destroy the part-illusory effect of velocity. The dictum 'never louder than beautiful' cannot be respected by the arhythmic ear, for the noise effect resulting from the unstable oscillations of a badly struck string is itself attributable to a mis-timed stroke. The expressive significance of varying lengths of staccato cannot be explored, and the role of the agogic accent remains undiscovered.

I am not suggesting that we should always approach music in a hypercritical and analytical state. There are times when, not as performers but as listeners, it is essential for us to be in a state of open sympathy with a musical work so that it can, indeed, 'creep in' upon us, and by joining with our own innate sense of music call forth a

---

[1] This is attributed by many psychologists to a deficiency in 'motor sense' rather than in actual aural endowment: the brain's power to organize temporal niceties being the relevant factor in this case.

E

response from our innermost selves. We train our pianistic technique in order to express our interpretation of music, and we train our ears to increase our appreciation and develop that personal 'chant intérieur' which informs our interpretation. Indeed an increased awareness of the musical meaning not only enhances our listening but illumines our performance.

In Appendix 1 the reader will find a section devoted to books on the cultivation of the ear, and he can pursue his own training with the assistance of a tape recorder or a musical friend if he is not in touch with a teacher. But the point of this chapter will have been missed if he does not, at the same time, make excursions into cognate subjects listed, such as harmony, form, style and interpretation, technique and pedalling, and so on, each new branch of music study lending depth and dimension to the rest.

If deaf mutes, as we are told, can respond to music through sensing and discriminating its vibrations, and enjoy its therapeutic value; what excuse can anyone of normal hearing have for remaining, through lack of application, in a half-deaf state musically? But, I would reiterate, ear-training exercises will be of limited use unless we also deepen our musical consciousness by increasing our musical knowledge and sensitivity generally—unless, indeed, we awaken the critic and artist within ourselves.

The lady who remonstrated with Turner that she could not see all the colours he had painted in his landscapes was justifiably re- buked for her lack of artistic participation by Turner's retort: 'Yes, but don't you wish you could?!'

II

Have I got 'Musical Talent'?

'Now there are varieties of gifts, but the same Spirit.'
(I Cor. xiii. 4)

You are a 'musical person' if you demonstrate a heightened awareness of music. As Professor Révész has stated:[1] 'Musicality denotes
primarily the ability to enjoy music aesthetically. Further, every
degree of profound understanding of musical form and the structure
of musical composition is based on musicality. A musical person has
a fine and developed instinct for the style and the rigid order of a
musical sequence of ideas. Another necessary characteristic of a
musical person is his capacity for becoming absorbed in the emo-
tions expressed by music and his ability to enter into so intimate a
relation with it, that the whole organization of his soul is affected
. . . Musicality is an innate and basic quality of the psychic organization of the person who possesses it, and it is a characteristic trait of
his individuality.'

Further, Mursell points out[2] that though musicality—defined
here as 'responsiveness to the tonal and rhythmic patterns which are
the substance of the art of music'—is well nigh universal, individuals
clearly differ in their innate sensitivity to musical stimuli, the purpose of all music training, then, being 'to bring about the evolution
of musical responsiveness', a purpose which remains the same at all
levels from the Kindergarten to the coaching of a concert artist.
At the same time it should be noted that executant dexterity in itself
is no indication of musicality. Artur Schnabel's[3] conscious preference for music that is 'better than it can be played' illustrates the

---

[1] *The Psychology of a Musical Prodigy* (Kegan Paul, 1925), p. 22.
[2] In *Basic Concepts in Music Education* (1958), p. 146.
[3] Cesar Saerchinger, *Artur Schnabel* (Cassell).

corollary—and perhaps prompted Leschetizky's remark: 'You will never be a pianist, you are a musician.'

But we nearly all possess a share of basic musicality. Indeed the congenitally unmusical are so few in number[1] as almost to constitute freaks of nature. For very probably the greater percentage of those who do appear to be unmusical have developed a constitutional non-musicality or anti-musicality for psychological reasons, which in some cases amount to a neurosis.

Révész[2] cites an interesting case history from Bernfeld in which 'a student who took a very active interest in music manifested nevertheless a certain lack of balance in his attitude towards it. Though he attended concerts assiduously he denied the fact to his friend. After the concerts he was often depressed. For years he had tried to master music, but nothing much came of his efforts. It was found that "objectively" he was not unmusical. For instance he could repeat melodies correctly, recognize dissonances, resolve chords, etc. In the course of his psycho-analytical treatment it was found that when a child of seven he had accidentally seen the violin-teacher kiss his elder sister. This situation, which formed the basis of a childish jealousy, had (according to psycho-analytical interpretation) awakened in him an insuperable hostility towards music which he could not overcome no matter how much he tried. The only thing left for him to do was to appear to be unmusical in order to justify his failure as a musician. Naturally the result of such an attitude is that the neurotically unmusical person gradually loses his musicality, and finally manifests all the characteristics of a congenitally unmusical person.'

Although one is increasingly disinclined today to accept the interpretations of psycho-analysts in all their detail, yet one cannot ignore the existence of many non-singers, for instance, hidebound in their conviction of possessing neither ear nor voice, whose incapa-

[1] Regarding the distribution of musical ability, Professor H. Lowery in *The Background of Music* writes: 'Whether we are justified in assuming that all individuals are musical in some degree is a question that has been frequently discussed and made the subject of experiment. Despite the variety of tests which have been used—some frankly auditory only, others depending upon the ability to sing or play, and others again demanding a working knowledge of musical grammar—the conclusion seems almost unanimous that the majority (it may be ninety per cent) of children do possess at least a rudimentary talent for music.'

[2] *Introduction to the Psychology of Music* (Longmans, 1952), p. 139.

city can be traced to some early humiliating experience when, as a 'growler' in an oversized school singing class they were sternly admonished to remain silent. These unfortunates regrettably for ever keep their peace! Smaller classes, and the time for more individual attention would have, in very many cases, disposed of the inability in childhood. Their later adult resistance to music has been developed as a defence mechanism: nothing more or less than a 'sour grapes' policy.

No, the fact that you are reading this book is itself an indication that you are very probably a musical person. For, as Révész[1] reminds us: 'Aptitudes manifest themselves principally in the form of direction of interest, and also in a marked educability and a rapid progress in the field indicated by the aptitude.' But, he warns, and it is a point on which I would lay the greatest emphasis, 'the greatest aptitude is not sufficient in itself if goal, plan, determination, zeal, passion, and study are not called into play at the right moment and in the right way. On the other hand, given a harmonious combination of spiritual and material circumstances *even a mediocre musical capacity is capable of outstanding accomplishment*.' (My italics)

Thus, having established the existence of our essential musicality (chapter 11), and discarded imagined handicaps (chapters 1, 6, 9, 10, 11); having analysed our motives (chapters 3, 4, 5) and set ourselves realistic aims (chapters 2, 7); having created congenial environmental conditions (chapters 1, 8), and employed the right methods to ensure progress (chapter 8 and appendices), we have but now to become PERSISTENT PIANISTS in order to succeed.

---

[1] Ibid., pp. 141, 142.

APPENDIX 1

Self-help

AN ANNOTATED BIBLIOGRAPHY

CONTENTS

INTRODUCTORY NOTE

In selecting the following books from my shelves to recommend to adult beginners I was tempted to review them in the usual manner. However, on recalling the numerous occasions in the past when I have been misled by a reviewer into purchasing a volume which on subsequent perusal proved useless for my purpose, I have adopted the unusual method of (where possible) confining myself to quoting from either the publisher's or author's own words in describing a particular work. This, I feel, gives a far more accurate guide to the book's contents and slant, as well as (in some cases) a taste of the author's individual style.

I hope that those adult beginners who live—as I do—in a district that is not blessed with generous music sections to either its public libraries or its book shops, will find the following pages a useful 'shoppers' guide'.

SELF-HELP RECORDS FOR WOULD-BE PIANISTS

The Pianist's Home Study Courses by James Ching, M.A., B.Mus.(Oxon), F.R.C.O. Available from Pianophone Tuition Ltd, 188 Vauxhall Bridge Rd, London S.W.1.

Course I (Beginners): 'To all those who wish to play the piano, but have not yet succeeded, this course is dedicated.'

Course II (More Advanced): 'For those who have always wanted to play better but have never been able to, this course is dedicated.'

Each course comprises (i) a *Master Music Book* containing exercises, studies, and pieces; (ii) *Instruction Booklets*; (iii) a 12-inch LP demonstration disc.

The James Ching Professional Service, 32 Cleveland Rd, S. Woodford, London, E.18.

Gramophone recordings and special annotations of the pianoforte music set in the local examinations of the Associated Board of the Royal Schools of Music.

Sidney Harrison Shows you How. Parlophone GEP 8579.

A demonstration and performance of Debussy, *Clair de Lune*, and Chopin, *Prelude in C Minor*, Op. 28, No. 20.

Antony Hopkins: Analytical Talks about Music, (with illustrations on the piano) in a series of 7-inch EP discs. Jupiter Recordings.

Bach: *Fugue No. 9* from the 2nd book of the '48'.   Jep OC19

(The Fugue is played in its entirety at the end of the analysis.)

Beethoven: *Piano Concerto No. 4*   Jep OC21
Rachmaninoff: *Piano Concerto No. 2.*   Jep OC13

POPULAR STYLE

Piano Jump, Play the piano by ear—NOW. Mark Robinson.
 (Piano Publicity Association, 26 Upper Brook St, London, W.I.)

BOOKS WRITTEN ESPECIALLY FOR THE AMATEUR PIANIST

Playing the Piano for Pleasure by Charles Cooke (Simon and Schuster, New York, 1941).

'The author of this book is one of the star reporters of *The New Yorker.* He is also a novelist. . . . Writing is his profession. Playing the piano is his hobby—a serious hobby. The result is, in effect, a book by an amateur addressed to other amateurs. It is written lightly, persuasively, humourously, inspiringly. It is full of concrete suggestions and instructions, based not only on the author's own experiences at the keyboard, but also on research conducted by interviewing such master pianists as Horowitz, Hoffman, Schnabel, Brailowsky, Arrau, and Rosenthal.' Publisher's Note.

The Amateur Pianist's Companion by James Ching, M.A., B.Mus.(Oxon) (Keith Prowse).

James Ching writes in his Foreword: ' . . . what almost every amateur wants is to be able to play well enough to give himself a reasonable amount of pleasure, satisfaction and even, perhaps, happiness by way of making enough progress to justify the amount of time he spends or at least is willing to spend. The surprising truth . . . is that nearly every amateur is actually capable of getting what he does want. . . . Provided, of course, that he is able and willing to study and practise intelligently for, say, an average of an hour a day for five days in the week and for forty odd weeks in the year. And provided also that, for most of the time at least, he occupies himself in doing the right things for the right reasons instead of, as usually happens, the wrong things for the wrong ones! Such, at least, has been the experience of the large numbers of amateur pianists who have . . . been studying at my school. Many of these, moreover, are men and women in the late forties, fifties and even sixties, who, as they have told me, seized upon my very revolutionary methods as something in the nature of a last chance for themselves.'

Note. This refers to Mr Ching's technical method whose exposition is given in his several works with great clarity and forthrightness. It is greatly at variance with the teachings of the 'relaxationist' school of Tobias Matthay (1858–1945), which have been widely used in this country, and whose famous exponents include Harriet Cohen, Myra Hess, and Irene Scharrer.

I omit to list Matthay's technical works because their involved style of writing reduces their value as self-help material.

Keys to the Keyboard by Andor Foldes (O.U.P., 1950).

The publishers write: 'This concise and informally written book, described by Sir Malcolm Sargent as a 'book of wisdom, well expressed and clear in its guidance', is primarily designed to help the amateur pianist who wants to get the most out of his piano playing. . . . Andor Foldes is an internationally known concert pianist. He was a pupil of Dohnanyi, and in this book he is able to pass on some of what he learned from his old master.'

The chapter headings are: (1) Getting the right start. (2) Reading and Listening. (3) Technique. (4) The Art of Practising. (5) Memorizing. (6) Getting ready to play in public. (7) Thoughts about Performing. (8) Questions and Answers about Piano Playing.

There is a useful Graded List of Playable Piano Music by Contemporary Composers compiled by John Lade.

Interpretation for the Piano Student by Joan Last (O.U.P., 1960).

'Practical advice on all the problems of interpretation and technique . . . from the middle grades up to Diploma standard.' For teachers, pupils and amateur pianists.

Miss Last writes in her Foreword: 'It must be realized that *grade* and *standard* in piano-playing are not one and the same thing, and it is a sad fact that, as the student passes through the grades, his standard often becomes lower. The further the aspiring pianist progresses the more it should become apparent to him that a good performance involves infinitely more than simply pushing down the right keys at the right moment. There are many who protest that they only play "for the fun of it", but I am sure that these people too will get far more fun from their music-making if the results are pleasant to listen to. . . .

'We are all students at heart, and whether we are learning to play, teach, or write there is always something new for us to discover. I have made endless discoveries through the difficulties of my own pupils. . . . These problems form the subject-matter of this book, and the suggestions which I have made as to their possible solution may be modified or augmented according to the experience of the reader.'

TWO BOOKS FOR ACCOMPANISTS

The Unashamed Accompanist by Gerald Moore (Methuen).

A delightful and informative book by this distinguished accompanist whose object is 'to induce more piano students or amateur pianists to take up accompanying for their careers or for their pleasure'.

Singer and Accompanist by Gerald Moore. 'The Performance of Fifty Songs' (Methuen, 1953).

'A book of extreme interest to singers and accompanists whether professional or amateur and to all lovers of music. It takes fifty songs at random (English, German, French, Spanish, Scandinavian, Russian) and with numerous illustrations explains how they should be sung and played.' Publisher's Note.

ON PRACTISING

The Secret of Successful Practice by E. Douglas Tayler, F.R.C.O., A.R.C.M. (Bosworth).

'May be used in conjunction with any recognized system.'

How to Practise by Hetty Bolton (Elkin).

'A Handbook for Pianoforte Students.'

Practising the Piano by Frank Merrick, F.R.C.M. (Rockliff, 1958).

'This book is the fruit of a lifetime of experience as a teacher and it has grown out of the advice which Mr Merrick has been in the habit of giving to his pupils. . . .

'It was at first Mr Merrick's opinion that a teacher ought to try to tell each pupil different things, since no two people are alike. But in the course of time he has accumulated an increasing number of precepts which have seemed valid for nearly all pupils coming under his care, and it is these precepts which make up the greater part of this book.' Publisher's Note.

NERVOUSNESS

Performer and Audience by James Ching, M.A., B.Mus.(Oxon) (Keith Prowse).

'An investigation into the psychological causes of Anxiety and Nervousness in Playing, Singing or Speaking before an Audience.'

STYLE AND INTERPRETATION: (A) MUSIC.

Style and Interpretation: an Anthology of Keyboard Music. Edited and annotated by Howard Ferguson (O.U.P., 1963/4).

Vol. 1: *Early Keyboard Music* (1) *England and France.* Anon., Byrd, Bull, Farnaby, Gibbons, Blow, Purcell, Arne, Chambonnières, d'Anglebert, F. Couperin, Rameau, Dandrieu and Daquin.

Vol. 2: *Early Keyboard Music* (2) *Germany and Italy.* Froberger, Handel, J. S. Bach, W. F. Bach, C. P. E. Bach, Frescobaldi and Scarlatti.

Vol. 3: *Classical Piano Music.* Haydn, Clementi, Mozart, Beethoven and Schubert.

Vol. 4: *Romantic Piano Music.* Field, Mendelssohn, Chopin, Schumann, Liszt and Brahms.

Dame Myra Hess writes in the Foreword: 'Students of the piano are often so preoccupied with the acquisition of technical skill that they do not give enough thought to stylistic, textual and interpretative considerations. This is a great mistake, for technique is only a stepping-stone and remains meaningless until it is allied to musical understanding. Innate musicality . . . must be cultivated, not only through contact with a wide variety of music, but through a knowledge of the way in which style and interpretation changes from century to century and country to country. . . . In the four volumes of this anthology Dr Ferguson has made an outstanding contribution to the clarification of these problems.'

An Introduction to the Performance of Bach by Rosalyn Tureck (O.U.P., 1960).

'A progressive anthology of keyboard music edited with introductory essays by Rosalyn Tureck.'

The music contained in the three books of this anthology has been re-recorded by Rosalyn Tureck on a 12-inch LP record entitled *An Introduction to Bach* for His Master's Voice (ALP 1747).

Forty-eight Preludes and Fugues. J. S. Bach. The Associated Board Edition edited by Donald Francis Tovey, fingered by Harold Samuel, 1924.

These include a general essay on the principles of interpretation of the Preludes and Fugues, together with individual analyses and notes on performance for each.

Beethoven Pianoforte Sonatas edited by D. F. Tovey and Harold Craxton, Associated Board Edition, 1931.

> Vol. 1 contains sonatas from Op. 2   No. 1, to Op. 22.
> Vol. 2   ,,   ,,   ,,   Op. 26   ,, Op. 54.
> Vol. 3   ,,   ,,   ,,   Op. 57   ,, Op. 111.

These volumes contain a general preface as well as separate notes on interpretation and performance for each sonata.

STYLE AND INTERPRETATION: (B) BOOKS

See *Interpretation for the Piano Student* by Joan Last (page 60).

The Secret of Musical Expression with special reference to Pianoforte Playing by E. Douglas Tayler, F.R.C.O., A.R.C.M. (Bosworth).

The author asks: 'How is one to set about playing with more expression? . . . a performance in which the player merely "does what he has been told" *can never be as effective as one based on intelligent study.*'

Piano Interpretation by Donald N. Ferguson (Williams & Norgate, 1950).

'Studies in the Music of Six Great Composers.'

The six composers are Beethoven, Schubert, Schumann, Chopin, Brahms, and Debussy.

'The author's aim is to present a clearer understanding of the problems of interpretations by constantly appealing to the reader's imagination. His stress, throughout the discussion of his chosen compositions, is on contour of melodic line, the nature of rhythm motion in music, the relation of melody and accompaniment, and the discovery of the composer's meaning through careful study of the text.' Publisher's Note.

MUSICAL FORM

Musical Form at the Piano by Alec Rowley and J. Raymond Tobin (J. Williams, 1942).

The authors write: 'Here . . . in one volume are pieces in Binary, Ternary, Simple Rondo, Extended Ternary, Air with Variations and Sonata (First Movement) form, so designed as to enable fingers, ear and eye to combine in assisting perception. . . . They are easy enough to be played by pianoforte students at an early state.'

Pattern Pieces by Frank Dawes (Curwen). 'An Introduction to Form.' An album of simple eighteenth- and nineteenth-century piano pieces, each with a formal analysis and graded list for further study.

Form in Pianoforte Music by C. Egerton Lowe (Hammond, 1932).

A handbook on musical analysis illustrated by reference to well-known pianoforte works.

Form in Music by Stewart Macpherson (J. Williams, revised edition, 1930).

A standard work on form in instrumental music.

J. S. Bach: Forty-eight Preludes and Fugues. Analysis of the Fugues by Orlando Morgan (Ashdown, 1931).

A Companion to Beethoven's Pianoforte Sonatas by Donald Francis Tovey (Associated Board, 1948).

'Bar-to-bar Analysis of all Beethoven's Pianoforte Sonatas, from the first note to the last.'

Bach's 48 Preludes and Fugues by Cecil Gray (O.U.P.).

THE CONCERTO

The Concerto, edited by Ralph Hill (Pelican, 1952).

'A guide to all the well-known piano, violin and cello concertos of the present-day repertoire. . . . The composers whose work is considered begin with Bach, and end with William Walton; special chapters are devoted to English compositions, to the general lines of development of the concerto, and to variation forms.'

Talking About Concertos by Antony Hopkins (Heinemann, 1964).

'Antony Hopkins is very well known—as composer, conductor, and (most widely) as a persuasive and entertaining broadcaster on music.'

The concertos chosen for analysis are: Mozart Piano Concertos in D minor and A major; Beethoven Piano Concertos No. 2 and No. 5 and Violin Concerto; Schumann Piano Concerto; Brahms Violin Concerto; Dvořák Violoncello Concerto; Rachmaninoff Piano Concerto No. 3; and Bartók Concerto for Orchestra.

CULTIVATING THE EAR

A Method of Aural Training by Eric Taylor (O.U.P., 1955).

The author writes in his preface: 'The trouble with aural tests is that we all think we can do them . . . However talented or untalented we may be, we can all improve our aural abilities by methodical practice. . . . This book . . . gives a basis for aural training which, while it is capable of, adaptation by individual students and teachers is methodical and complete. . . . It is not intended to replace or compete with "official" specimen ear tests: on the contrary it is meant to provide the general background which they will test. Part I will serve as a basis for examinations up to and including Grade V of both the Associated Board and Trinity College local examinations; Part II extends to Grade VII of the Associated Board and Trinity College, and also the Ordinary Level of most Universities' G.C.E. Part III covers the Grade VIIIs, G.C.E. at Advanced Level, and the Diploma examinations—L.R.A.M., A.T.C.L., L.T.C.L., L.R.S.M., A.R.C.O., etc.'

Aural Tests by Basil C. Allchin and Ernest Read (revised by William Cole) (Associated Board).

Specimen Tests for the guidance of teachers and candidates preparing for the examinations of the Royal Schools of Music.

Part 1: Grades I, II, III, IV, V.

Part 2: Grades VI and VII.

Part 3: Grade VIII.

Part 4: Diploma Examinations (L.R.A.M., A.R.C.M., L.R.S.M.).

Self-help in Aural Tests: Pitch (Intervals). by J. Raymond Tobin (Joseph Williams, 1948).

'One of the things which hinder progress in aural work is that we do too much *testing* and too little aural *practice*.'

The Music-Lover's Ear Tests and Book of Themes by E. Markham Lee (Banks & Son, 1932).

Part I: Easy (up to and including Grade V).

Part II: More advanced (up to diploma standards).

Tests in intervals, rhythm, under melodies, cadences, and modulations are here linked with definite well-known music. The book draws on some hundreds of extracts from standard and classical works for the tests, and includes hints on their preparation and methods of study.

The Music-Lover's Sight Singing Tests and Book of Themes by E. Markham Lee (Banks & Son, 1937).

Sight-singing helps to correlate eye and ear, and is useful for the pianist as well as the singer for whom this book is primarily intended. It contains 150 melodies from classic and standard sources.

Sight-Singing Tests by I. Rees-Davies (Novello's Music Primers No. 108).

A collection of graded sight-singing tests, with general hints on sight-singing, leading up to the standard required for Diplomas in Appreciation, Aural Training and Voice Culture of the Royal Academy and Royal College.

The Authentic Two-Part Aural Practice Book by Dorothy Bradley (Ricordi).

'Many candidates find considerable difficulty in performing the two-part aural tests set for the Associated Board L.R.A.M., A.R.C.M., A.R.C.O., and other examinations. The very first factor in approaching this problem is *concentration*, the second is *confidence*, all the rest is a matter of practice.'

Note. Any pianist who hopes to perform music of a contrapuntal texture (such as a Bach fugue) with any success must have the ability to listen to *all* the moving parts.

ON MEMORIZING

Memory Playing at the Piano by J. Raymond Tobin (Joseph Williams, 1944).

'A "first" book of how to memorize, with musical illustrations.'

In his Foreword the author writes: 'The pieces in this book are simple and straightforward. . . . Each contains enough variety of theme, tonality, etc., to train and test powers of memory. All are short, so that confidence may be readily attained. The explanatory notes, which face each piece, give the mind something to which it may hold fast, during performance without the copy. . . . The power to play by memory can be, and should be, developed and organized by every student: for the piece that is not known from memory is not throughly known.'

Music by Heart by Lilias Mackinnon.

The publishers write: 'As its title indicates, this is a book primarily concerned with the memorizing of music. But its scope is far wider than this. . . . Nerves, the relation between memory and technique, the working of the subconscious mind, relaxation and fatigue—all these subjects and a multitude of others with which Miss Mackinnon deals are of the greatest importance to every performer and teacher.'

Leff Pouishnoff writes: 'It will prove of great value to students of music and will help them to overcome the fear of forgetting.'

Musical Memory and its Cultivation by Frederick G. Shinn (Vincent, 1898).

This is probably the earliest work on the subject of memory in its connection with music and musical performance. In it Shinn stresses the importance of cultivating a memory for musical sounds and performance rather as a valuable educational tool than as an incitement for all to play 'without the book'. He analyses and shows the application of muscular, visual, and intellectual memory in pianoforte music, and has an interesting chapter on some phenomenal memories possessed by famous musicians.

SIGHT-READING

Sight-Reading at the Piano by Alec Rowley, F.R.A.M., F.R.C.O., F.T.C.L. The step-by-step series of Practical Musicianship Booklets (Joseph Williams, 1936. In 3 stages).

Alec Rowley writes in his Foreword: 'The booklets . . . are based upon the modern teaching practice of *learning by doing*. They are written in plain, direct language. All, young or old, who can play a simple melody on the pianoforte, can begin to sight-read at the keyboard. The value of Sight-Reading is so obvious that the point need not be laboured, but we know by experience how few there are who have mastered this important branch of musicianship.'

Sight-Reading Made Easy by Dorothy Bradley and J. Raymond Tobin (J. Williams, 1947. Books 1–8).

'A complete graded course for the pianoforte.' The authors write in their Foreword: 'The object of this new series is to train the student: (1) to observe essential details; (2) to cultivate the power of concentration and the ability to remember; (3) to develop skill in "snap-shotting" small sections and phrases, and to aid accurate performance; (4) to form a habit of preparing the fingers over the keys in readiness for any fingering group likely to occur in the particular grade; (5) to read by interval and to play by feel; to be independent in keyboard location and confident in attack.'

These books give practical hints throughout, and guide the student towards the right mental approach to sight-reading. The grading corresponds with Associated Board, Trinity College, and other examining bodies.

Rhythmic Reading by Joan Last. Books I–V (Bosworth, 1953, etc.).

Well-graded material, related in standard to the requirements of the Associated Board examinations.

MELODY MAKING AT THE KEYBOARD

Melody Making at the Piano by Alec Rowley and J. Raymond Tobin. The step by step series of Practical Musicianship Booklets (J. Williams, 1937. In 3 stages).

'At the outset, only the five white keys from "Middle C" are used. These five keys lie under the hand and their sounds are either familiar or readily become so. Yet their range is sufficient to show the meaning and application of *phrase, balance, climax* and the making, placing and effect of *cadences.* . . .

'The making of melodies at the keyboard, as here presented, is the first simple step in the art of Improvisation.'—Authors' Foreword.

Also see *Book I, Melody Making*, of Angela Diller's Keyboard Harmony Course (p. 69).

MODULATION AT THE KEYBOARD

Modulation at the Piano by J. Raymond Tobin, Mus.B. The step by step series of Practical Musicianship Booklets (J. Williams, 1937. In 3 stages).

'Keyboard modulation will ensure ease and accuracy in the reading of music. It will establish a sense of key, increase familiarity with all keys, stimulate musical initiative, help creative work (melody-making, cadence-playing etc.) and lead to discrimination in the use of chords.

'The booklets begin at the beginning, and all—young or old—can acquire (1) the power to pass from key to key at the instrument, and (2) the ability to follow the course of keys in any printed music.

'The only previous knowledge actually demanded is familiarity with the

F

signatures of simple keys (in Stages 1 and 2, not exceeding three flats or three sharps) and the ability to play a simple melody.' From Author's Foreword.

TRANSPOSITION AT THE KEYBOARD

Transposing at the Piano by J. Raymond Tobin. The step by step series of Practical Musicianship Booklets (J. Williams, 1937. In 3 stages).

'Simple keyboard transposition provides a better way than interminable scale-playing to the gaining of a knowledge of keys. It gives a ready knowledge, and through constant "awareness" of the notes builds up a strong key-sense. It makes all reading at sight easier, prevents the natural ear from being spoiled or blunted by pitch errors, and creates a firm link between *sign* and *sound*.' From Author's Foreword.

Transposition at the Keyboard by Ieuan Rees-Davies (Curwen Edition No. 8334).

The author writes: 'The would-be transposer must learn to *hear mentally* what is expressed on the printed page, and then, with the knowledge and experience of other keys, be able to express at another pitch exactly what the mind has retained.'

KEYBOARD HARMONY

Harmonization at the Piano by Alec Rowley and J. Raymond Tobin. The step by step series of Practical Musicianship Booklets (Joseph Williams, 1937. In 3 stages).

The authors write: 'These booklets present *Harmony* and *Harmonization of Melodies* by the practical method of "learning by doing". . . . They show by simple word and example what can be done: and deal only with points which can be, and are, applied immediately at the keyboard.

'The ear and the hand on the keyboard are used as constant guide and argument. . . .

'A rudimentary knowledge of keys and intervals is presupposed.'

Keyboard Harmony for Beginners by J. Barham Johnson (O.U.P., 1947).

The author writes:

'The scope of this book is definite, though limited, and its plan is simple.

'It is designed for (1) the absolute beginner at the piano; (2) the elementary pianist who has never studied harmony; (3) pupils who have done paper-work but need to put their knowledge to practical use and aural test.

'The plan of the book is to treat each of five major and minor keys (up to two sharps and two flats) separately and exhaustively. Each new problem is isolated and dealt with until throughly known. Each set of exercises is followed by tunes, summing up the particular points studied.'

Keyboard Harmony and Improvisation by Kenneth Simpson (Lengnick, 1963).

'This book, the outcome of a good many years' experience of helping pupils and students of various ages and talents to approach this subject, offers, by means of carefully graded and abundant exercises, a way of acquiring systematically the resource needed to harmonize most of the tunes found in well-known song books, and to add appropriate harmonic clothing to original melodies.' From Author's Preface.

Keyboard Harmony Course by Angela Diller (Chappell).

Book 1: Melody Making (1936).
Book 2: Harmonic development and Chord Vocabulary.
Book 3: Harmonizing Melodies with an elementary chord vocabulary (1943).
Book 4: Harmonizing Melodies and Analysing Illustrative Material (1949).

'These books are written with the purpose of giving students a practical first-hand experience of how music is made, not by theorizing about it, but by immediately making it.

'Many students who can play difficult pieces are unable to make up tunes, or to play simple tunes by ear, or to play chords to accompany a simple melody, or to transpose pieces into other keys, or to modulate on the piano from one key to another. They are inclined to think that these are things that only especially gifted people can do. But they are really things that *anyone* with intelligence, and the will and the patience to learn, can accomplish.' From Author's Preface.

Keyboard approach to harmony by Margaret Lowry, M.A. (Theodore Presser Co., Pennsylvania, 1949).

The author writes: 'This book . . . seeks to give an easy familiarity with the most common idioms of our musical speech. . . . This text is not intended to replace any part of advanced training but might be considered rather as a preview of basic harmony, a foundation on which more specialized skills may be built with fluency and understanding. . . .

'This material . . . has been found extremely helpful as supplementary work for students who have had the usual training and yet lack ability to employ the simple tools of harmony easily.'

IMPROVISATION

See Melody Making at the Keyboard, p. 67.

Adventures in Improvisation by Frederick Nicholls and J. Raymond Tobin (J. Williams, 1937).

Extract from authors' Foreword: 'This book is designed to assist students to cultivate the useful faculty of improvisation. It offers a simple, definite plan for building-up short movements from two or three chords, and yet it stimulates musical initiative and gives scope for self-expression and individual imagination.

'With rare exceptions, the chords used are simple triads of the key, but the wider the harmonic resource of the student, the greater the variety and artistry which are possible. . . .

'The last few adventures will be found particularly useful as tests in preparation for the improvisation tests in the examinations for the Royal College of Organists and Trinity College of Music (musicianship) Diplomas.'

How to Improvise Piano Accompaniments by J. Raymond Tobin (O.U.P., 1956).

'The simple specimen formulae given in these pages will be found easy to carry in the head and to keep at the finger tips. Only four particular skills are considered: (1) The ability to play a suitable pianoforte accompaniment for scales in any key which may be required. . . . (2) The ability to play a few suitable chords while the voice sustains a long sound, to give the necessary instrumental and harmonic support or to invest the exercise with rhythmic sense or drive. (3) The ability to play a succession of single sounds or of chords which will effect an orderly modulation (change of key) from any key to any other key, as required or desired. . . . (4) The ability to provide an outline or very simple piano accompaniment to familiar songs (nursery, folk, national) at times when only a "melody" edition is available.' From Author's Preface.

PRACTICAL MUSICIANSHIP (GENERAL)

Graded Tests in Practical Musicianship and Musical Initiative by Alec Rowley and J. Raymond Tobin. The step by step series of Practical Musicianship Booklets (J. Williams, 1937. In 3 books).

'Practical Musicianship Tests . . . provide mental, muscular, aural and visual training . . . The sets of questions are graded, and each set is progressively arranged. They cover *location, rhythm, tonality, melody-making, phrasing, form, transposition* and *modulation*. The earlier sets are suitable for the . . . beginner, whose introduction to the keyboard is but recent.' From Authors' Foreword.

PIANO TECHNIQUE

See (1) James Ching's *The Amateur Pianist's Companion* (p. 59), and (2) *Practising the Piano* by Frank Merrick (p. 61).

Piano Technique by Sidney Harrison (Pitman, 1953).

'Sidney Harrison is unusually well qualified to write on the technique of piano playing. Not only has he had long experience as a teacher and as an adjudicator at musical festivals, but he has achieved outstanding success as a television broadcaster by his ability to explain technical matters in a simple and straightforward manner.' Publisher's note.

Mr Harrison writes in his Preface: 'Since technique is a means to an end I have inevitably had to relate the control of touch and tone to questions of phrasing and expression. . . . I have tried to be clear and practical, but not dogmatic.'

The Technique of Piano Playing by József Gát, translated by István Kleszky (Corvina, Budapest, 1958).

Imre Ungár writes: 'It is not the speed of the fingers that is equivalent to good technique: it is the ability to make the piano weep and smile, to evoke human and artistic feelings and manifestations. A particular merit of the book is to have investigated, with absolute precision, all pertinent facts and data.'

A monumental work: quite the most fascinating book on piano technique I have been privileged to read.

MUSCULAR EXERCISES (away from the keyboard)

Aids to Technique by Eric Hope (Ashdown, 1962).

'Muscular development exercises for pianists and other instrumentalists.'

Hand Gymnastics by Ridley Prentice (Novello).

'For the scientific development of the muscles used in pianoforte playing.' Exercises are included for the arm, wrist, for stretching the hand, for the fingers (knuckle joints, middle joints, end joints) and for the thumb.

Note. Muscular exercises away from the piano are made use of in Ching's *Pianophone Tuition Course* (see p. 58); and there is a chapter on them in Gát's *The Technique of Piano Playing* (see above).

TECHNICAL EXERCISES (at the keyboard)

Hand Development Exercises for Pianoforte by Henry Geehl (Bosworth).

'For increasing the span of the hand and fingers.'

Foundations of Pianoforte Technique by Geoffrey Tankard, Professor, Royal College of Music, London (Elkin).

'Comprehensive technical exercises with directions as to "how" and "what" to avoid', graded from Grade II to Grade VIII. These can be followed by:

Pianoforte Technique on an Hour a Day by Geoffrey Tankard and Eric Harrison (Elkin). Grade VII to Concert Level. A chart is included which suggests how to allocate with the greatest advantage the time available for practising technique.

New School of Fundamental Pianoforte Technics by Walter Fickert (Bosworth)

'A work containing all the necessary basic technical exercises preparatory to the actual study of Etudes,' based on a research into the practice of a number of prominent teachers.

THE USE OF THE PEDALS: (A) Exercises and studies for the beginner

First Pedal-Studies for the Piano by Angela Diller and Elizabeth Quaile (Chappell, 1942).

'24 progressive exercises and pieces.'

The New Graded Pedalling by James Ching (Keith Prowse. Two books).

Containing 'plenty of carefully graded exercises and pieces of particular musical interest. . . . It can be used with success by first and second year students also by others more advanced whose control of the pedal is not at par with their keyboard technique.'

THE USE OF THE PEDALS: (B) Guides for students

Points on Pedalling by James Ching (Forsyth, 1930).

Mr Ching writes in his Foreword: 'In spite of the fact that really fine pedalling must ultimately depend, just as any other branch of interpretation does, upon musical experience and judgement; nevertheless the foundations of most forms of pedalling can be taught by fairly definite rules, and this is perhaps the surest way in which the necessary experience and judgement can be acquired.'

Pedalling the Modern Pianoforte by York Bowen (O.U.P., 1936).

The author writes: 'Pedalling is an art that has only recently been considered with the comprehensive and detailed analysis that it deserves. . . . If the perusal of this book leads to a better understanding of some of the vital things in this art—and to better results—then . . . my mission will have been fulfilled.'

TWO IMPORTANT BOOKS FOR PIANISTS

Men, Women and Pianos by Arthur Loesser (Gollancz, 1955).

The publishers write: 'Mr Loesser has had no less ambitious an idea than that of taking the piano as a centre for writing the social history of the last three hundred years; and he has, we think, risen magnificently to his own challenge.'

The Great Pianists by Harold C. Schonberg (Gollancz, 1964).

This book, written by the music critic of the *New York Times*, deals with the great pianists (and many more)—'their lives, their techniques, their theories, their particular contributions to the piano, their individual claims to greatness. . . . The conflict of styles and methods is traced from era to era and fashion to fashion.'

MUSIC: GENERAL KNOWLEDGE

An ABC of Music by Imogen Holst (O.U.P., 1963).

'This book is designed to provide a general survey of all musical terms and ideas which are likely to be met with by the amateur musician. It is, in fact, a short, practical guide to the basic essentials of rudiments, harmony, and form. . . . It is an excellent introduction to the language of music.

'Imogen Holst, daughter of Gustav Holst, is herself a composer, and the author of a number of books on music.'

The Oxford Companion to Music by Percy A. Scholes (O.U.P., First published in 1938, 9th edition 1955).

An authoritative, comprehensive and scholarly work on all aspects of music, compiled as a self-indexed, cross-referenced encyclopedia.

A nucleus for your music library.

A Course in Musical Composition by Norman Demuth (Bosworth).

Part I. Technique, Idiom, Style. 1950.
Part II. Variation, The Suite. 1953.
Part III. Form, The Sonata. 1955.
Part IV. The Overture, Symphonic Poem, Concerto. 1955.

'I assume for the purpose of this book that the student-composer will have mastered the basic technique of present-day text-book harmony and counterpoint and the question of tonality and key-relationship. I take it for granted that he will have creative instincts and musical feeling; but *A Course in Musical Composition* does not preclude the study of *THE Course OF Musical Composition*, and for this reason the general reader will find that he will be able to follow the natural evolution of each genre in these pages.' From Author's Foreword.

JAZZ

The Jazz Scene by Francis Newton (Pelican).

'In *The Jazz Scene* Francis Newton probes deeper than the usual potted histories. He examines not only the origins of jazz but the business set-up, the jazz public, jazz vogues in Britain, and the influences of jazz on serious and "pop" music.' Publisher's Note.

APPENDIX 2

Repertoire

'Tell me what you like and I will tell you the kind of man you are.' Ruskin

I. MUSIC AT THE HALF-WAY HOUSE

GRADE IV

Prelude in D Minor, No. 3 of *Six Little Preludes*	J. S. Bach
Minuet I from *French Suite No. 3* in B Minor	J. S. Bach
Gavotte from *French Suite No. 5* in G	J. S. Bach
Allegro (First Movement), *Sonata in C*, K.545	Mozart
Minuet in G	Beethoven
Für Elise (Albumblatt)	Beethoven
Bagatelle in F, Op. 33 No. 3	Beethoven
Bagatelle in D, Op. 33 No. 6	Beethoven
Sonata in G, Op. 49 No. 2	Beethoven
Ecossaise in B Minor	Schubert
To Music	Schubert, arranged Gerald Moore (Oxford)
Knight Rupert (*Album for the Young*, Op. 68 No. 12)	Schumann
Of Strange Lands and People (*Scenes from Childhood*, Op. 15 No. 1)	Schumann
Nos. 8 and 11 from *Kleine Klavierstücke*	César Franck (Peters Edition 4529)
Album Leaf (*Lyric Pieces*, Book I, Op. 12 No. 7)	Grieg
National Song (*Lyric Pieces*, Book I, Op. 12 No. 8)	Grieg
An Autumn Tale	Ivor Foster (Associated Board)
Minuet for a Modern Grandmother (Grade IV 1963 Associated Board Examination Pieces)	Shena Fraser

GRADE V

Gigue in G Minor (La Milordine)	Couperin
Two Part Invention No. 13 in A Minor	J. S. Bach
Prelude in C, Book I No. 1 of the 48 Preludes and Fugues	J. S. Bach
Sanctify us by Thy Goodness (from Cantata No. 22)	J. S. Bach, arranged Harriet Cohen (O.U.P.)
Countess of Westmoreland's Delight	Shield, arranged Moffat (Augener)
Finale (Allegro) from Sonata No. 5 in C	Haydn

Finale (Presto ma non troppo) from Sonata No. 7 in D	Haydn
Second Movement (Adagio) from Sonata in F, K.280	Mozart
Minuets 1 and 2 from Sonata in E flat, K.282	Mozart
Minuet and Trio from Sonata in F, K.331	Mozart
Bagatelle in G Minor, Op. 119 No. 1	Beethoven
Bagatelle in C, Op. 119 No. 2	Beethoven
First Movement (Andante) from Sonata in G Minor, Op. 49 No. 1	Beethoven
Second Movement (Andante) from Sonata in G, Op. 79	Beethoven
Venetian Gondola Song (*Songs without words*, Op. 19 No. 6	Mendelssohn
The Horseman (*Album for the Young*, Op. 68 No. 23)	Schumann
A Strange Story (*Scenes from Childhood*, Op. 15 No. 2)	Schumann
Quite Happy (*Scenes from Childhood*, Op. 15 No. 5)	Schumann
Prelude in E Minor, Op. 28 No. 4	Chopin
Prelude in A, Op. 28 No. 7	Chopin
Prelude in C Minor, Op. 28 No. 20	Chopin
Waltz in A Minor, Op. 34 No. 2	Chopin
Waltz in B Minor, Op. 69 No. 2	Chopin
Nocturne in E flat, Op. 9 No. 2	Chopin
Little Bird (*Lyric Pieces*, Book 3)	Grieg
Holy Boy	John Ireland (Boosey and Hawkes)

2. A REPERTOIRE FOR THE PERSISTENT PIANIST

Music in the three highest amateur grades

GRADE VI

Le Bavolet flottant	Couperin
Prelude in F Minor, Book 2 No. 12 of the 48 Preludes and Fugues	J. S. Bach
Sheep may safely graze (from the Birthday Cantata)	J. S. Bach, transcribed Mary Howe (O.U.P.)
Jesu, Joy of man's desiring (Chorale from Cantata No. 147)	J. S. Bach, arranged Myra Hess (O.U.P.)

Solfegietto	C. P. E. Bach
Toccata in A	Paradies
Presto (First Movement), Sonata No. 2 in E Minor	Haydn
Allegro (First Movement), Sonata in G, K.283	Mozart
Fantasia I in D Minor, K.397	Mozart
Minuet and Trio from Sonata in B flat, Op. 22	Beethoven
Presto (First Movement), Sonata in G, Op. 79	Beethoven
Bagatelle in A Minor, Op. 119 No. 9	Beethoven
Adagio Cantabile (Second Movement), Sonata in C Minor, Op. 13, 'Pathétique'	Beethoven
Moment Musical in F Minor, Op. 94 No. 3	Schubert
Song without words, Op. 62 No. 3 in E Minor	Mendelssohn
Prelude in D flat, Op. 28 No. 15	Chopin
Prelude in B Minor, Op. 28 No. 6	Chopin
Nocturne in G Minor, Op. 37 No. 1	Chopin
Nocturne in F Minor, Op. 55 No. 1	Chopin
Waltzes: E Minor (Posthumous); A flat, Op. 69 No. 1; F Minor, Op. 70 No. 2	Chopin
Mazurkas: G Minor, Op. 24 No. 1; C, Op. 67 No. 3	Chopin
The Entreating Child (*Scenes from Childhood,* Op. 15 No. 4)	Schumann
Dreaming (*Scenes from Childhood,* Op. 15 No. 7)	Schumann
Child falling asleep (*Scenes from Childhood,* Op. 15 No. 12)	Schumann
Waltz in C sharp Minor, Op. 39 No. 7	Brahms
Butterfly (*Lyric Pieces,* Book 3), Op. 43 No. 1	Grieg
Poetic Tone Picture, Op. 3, No. 1	Grieg
Little Shepherd (*Children's Corner* Suite, No. 5)	Debussy (U.M.P.)
Le Pastour, No. 6; and *Petites Litanies de Jésus,* No. 8 (*L'Almanach aux Images*)	Gabriel Grovlez (Augener)
Musical Box (*En Vacances,* No. 6)	de Severac (Editions Salabert, U.M.P.)
Rosemary	Frank Bridge (Boosey)

GRADE VII

Sonatas Nos. 2 and 5 (Augener, Book I)	Scarlatti
Le Coucou	Daquin
Prelude in G, Book 1 No. 15 of the 48 Preludes and Fugues	J. S. Bach

Allegro con brio (First Movement), Sonata No. 7
   in D   Haydn

Allegro (First Movement), Sonata in C Minor,
   K.457   Mozart

Allegro (First Movement), Sonata in F Minor,
   Op. 2 No. 1   Beethoven

Largo e mesto (Second Movement), Sonata in D,
   Op. 10 No. 3   Beethoven

Allegro (First Movement) and *Vivace* (Third
   Movement), Sonata in G, Op. 14 No. 2   Beethoven

Adagio sostenuto (First Movement), Sonata in
   C sharp Minor, Op. 27, 'The Moonlight'   Beethoven

Bagatelle in A flat, Op. 33 No. 7   Beethoven

Impromptu in A flat, Op. 90 No 4   Schubert

Songs Without Words, Op. 38 No. 2 in C Minor;
   Op. 67 No. 5 in B Minor; Op. 102 No. 3 in C   Mendelssohn

Prelude in G Minor, Op. 28 No. 22   Chopin

Waltz in C sharp Minor, Op. 64 No. 2   Chopin

Mazurka in A Minor, Op. 68 No. 2   Chopin

Arabesque, Op. 18   Schumann

Waltz in A flat, Op. 39 No. 15   Brahms

Rhapsody in G Minor, Op. 79   Brahms

Nocturne (*Lyric Pieces*, Book 5), Op. 54 No. 4   Grieg

Two Arabesques   Debussy (U.M.P.)

Andaluza   Granados (Chester)

The Little White Donkey   Jacques Ibert (U.M.P.)

GRADE VIII

Forlorn Hope   John Dowland,
                             Ed. Peter Warlock
                             (Curwen)

Pastorale and Capriccio   Scarlatti–Tausig

Fantasia in C Minor   J. S. Bach

First Movement (Allegro), Italian Concerto   J. S. Bach

Allemande, Courante, Sarabande, Loure and Gigue,
   French Suite No. 5 in G   J. S. Bach

Prelude and Fugue in C Minor, Book I No. 2 of
   the 48 Preludes and Fugues   J. S. Bach

Prelude and Fugue in D, Book I No. 5 of the 48
   Preludes and Fugues   J. S. Bach

Rondo in A Minor, K.511   Mozart

Fantasia in C Minor, K. 475	Mozart
Variations in F Minor (Andante con variazioni)	Haydn
Rondo in G, Op. 51 No. 2	Beethoven
Rondo (Allegretto), Last Movement, Sonata in B flat, Op. 22	Beethoven
Sonata in E, Op. 14 No. 1 (Allegro, Allegretto, Rondo)	Beethoven
Sonata in F sharp, Op. 78 (Adagio Cantabile, Allegro ma non troppo, Allegro vivace)	Beethoven
Impromptu in B flat, Op. 142 No. 3	Schubert
The Prophet Bird (*Forest Scenes*, Op. 82 No. 7)	Schumann
Impromptu in A flat, Op. 29	Chopin
Fantaisie Impromptu, Op. 66	Chopin
Etude in A flat, Op. 25 No. 1 (The Shepherd Boy/The Aeolian Harp)	Chopin
Liebesträume, No. 3 in A flat	Liszt
Intermezzo in A, Op. 118 No. 2	Brahms
Berceuse from *Dolly* Suite, Op. 56	Franck (U.M.P.)
Sevillanas	Albeniz (J. Williams)
Seguidillas	Albeniz (Chester)
La fille aux cheveux de lin	Debussy
Clair de Lune	Debussy
Golliwog's cake walk (*Children's Corner* Suite)	Debussy
Menuet from *Le Tombeau de Couperin*	Ravel
Pavane pour une Infante Défunte	Ravel
Prelude in G Minor, Op. 23 No. 5	Rachmaninoff
Prelude in G, Op. 32 No. 5	Rachmaninoff
Refrain de Berceau	Palmgren
The Darkened Valley	John Ireland

3. AN INTRODUCTION TO CONTEMPORARY MUSIC

Many people believe that contemporary music is both difficult to listen to and difficult to play, and very many pianoforte teachers do not introduce it to their pupils.

At a recent gathering of several hundred pianoforte teachers, those willing to teach music written in contemporary idioms were asked to raise their hands. I was able to count those responding on my own two!

Of the adult beginners replying to questionnaires, one had performed the service of introducing contemporary music to her teacher; while nearly all stated that they preferred Classical and Romantic pieces. Mozart,

Beethoven, and Chopin headed the list of 'favourite composers', and Bach and Schubert came next.

However one contemporary music enthusiast wrote: 'The music club recitals often include a short modern piece (usually of a comic nature!) but I mainly rely on the B.B.C. for getting to know more modern music. . . . I rather hope you might be able to do something for the adult beginner who is not content with the usual very simple classics that seem to come my way too often!'

To this adult beginner then, but more particularly to those who have been misled by a conspiracy of silence into believing that anything after Debussy (Bartók occasionally excepted) has been written by musical charlatans, I would introduce the following.

New Directions: Approaches to contemporary idioms, by George Anson (Chappell).

Contains short pieces, about Grades I and II, with short explanatory texts on Atonality, Polytonality, Twelve-Note Row, Linear Counterpoint, Note-Clusters, Barless Music, Changing Metres, etc.

Travel Diaries by Malcolm Williamson (Chappell).

Include notes on technique and interpretation for each piece. (1) Sydney (Easy). (2) Naples (Easy to Moderately Easy). (3) London (Moderately Easy). (4) Paris (Moderately Difficult). (5) New York (Difficult).

GRADE I

From the memories of Auntie Catinca (No. 2 of *Poze si Pozne*) by Mihail Jora (The Rumanian Legation, 4 Palace Gardens, W.8).
Sadness (from *Twelve American Preludes*) by Alberto Ginastera (Carl Fischer Inc., 56–62 Cooper Sq., New York 3, N.Y.).
Children's Dance by Zoltán Kodály (Boosey and Hawkes).
Duettino (from *The New Piano Book*, Vol. I) by Philip Jarnach (Schott).
Bagpipes and *Oxen* (from *Cats' Chorus*) by Joan Rimmer (Lengnick).
The Hen in the Garden (from *Jardin d'enfants*) by Simone Plé (U.M.P.).

GRADES I–II

Selected pieces from *Five by Ten* Grade I (Very Easy to Easy) edited by Alec Rowley, Lengnick. (Not at all outré. Recommended to adult beginners of more conservative taste.)

    No. 10 Madeleine Dring, 'Roundelay'
    No. 12 Edmund Rubbra, 'Hurdy Gurdy'

No. 16 Madeleine Dring, 'Courtiers' Dance'
No. 19 Franz Reizenstein, 'The First Snowdrop'
No. 22 William Alwyn, 'The Village Bell-Ringers'
No. 25 William Alwyn, 'What the Mill Wheel told me'

GRADE II

Melodia (from *Hybrids*) by Ferenc Farcas (Mills Music Ltd).
Ballo Gaio (from *Reihe Kleiner Klavierstücke*) by Henk Badings (Schott).
Rumanian Christmas Carol by Bartók (Universal Edition).
Moujik, Camels, and *Train* (from *Cats' Chorus*) by Joan Rimmer (Lengnick).

GRADES II–III

Selected pieces from *Five by Ten* Grade II (Easy to Moderately Easy) edited
by A. Rowley (Lengnick). For conservative tastes.

No. 1 Julius Harrison, 'Autumn Days'
No. 2 Elizabeth Machonchy, 'Cradle Song'
No. 5 Madeleine Dring, 'The Horse Rider'
No. 15 Charles Proctor, 'The Wooden Soldier'
No. 19 Madeleine Dring, 'Minuet'

No. 2 of *Six Rumanian Folk Dances* by Béla Bartók (Universal Edition
5802).
In Yugoslav Mode by Béla Bartók. No. 40 of *Mikrokosmos*, Vol. II (Boosey
and Hawkes)

GRADE III

Marsch (from *Wir bauen eine Stadt*) by Paul Hindemith (Schott).
Lento (from *Les Cinq Doigts*) by Igor Stravinsky (Chester).
Pastorale by Arnold Cooke (Ricordi).
Keringo (Waltz) by Béla Bartók (Chesterian Series Grade III No. 7, Chester).
Puppet's Waltz by Christopher Wiltshire (Associated Board).
Notturno (from *Hybrids*) by Ferenc Farcas (Mills Music Ltd).

GRADES III–IV

Selected pieces from *Miniaturen* by Sabin V. Dragoi (Lengnick, Simrock
edition 3049).

No. 4 'The Shepherd'
No. 5 'Old Folk Dance'
No. 6 'Someone who does not love'
No. 7 'Spring Dance'
No. 8 'The Mill'

Selected pieces from *Nine Easy Piano Pieces*, Op. 54, by Sergei Bortkiewicz (Lengnick). For more conservative tastes.

    No. 1 'Russian Peasant Girl'
    No. 2 'The Cossack'
    No. 3 'The Spanish Lady'
    No. 5 'The Gipsy'

GRADE IV

Morning (from *One Day*) by Darius Milhaud (Schott).

No. 4 of *Six Rumanian Folk Dances* by Béla Bartók (Universal Edition 5802).

Clock-work Doll (from *Six Children's Pieces*) by Shostakovich (Boosey and Hawkes).

Saturday's Child (from *A Week of Birthdays*) by Richard Rodney Bennett (Mills Music Ltd).

GRADES IV–V

Selected pieces from *Five by Ten* Grade III (Moderately Easy to Moderate) edited by Alec Rowley (Lengnick).

    No. 2 Madeleine Dring, 'Sad Princess'
    No. 3 Edmund Rubbra, 'Peasant Dance'
    No. 10 Franz Reizenstein, 'An Echo Tune'
    No. 11 Julius Harrison, 'Caprice'
    No. 12 Franz Reizenstein, 'A Walking Tune'

Jig for Pianoforte by Madeleine Dring (Lengnick).

GRADE V

Visions Fugitives, Op. 22 No. 6, by Prokofiev (Boosey and Hawkes).

Bagatelle (No. 4 of *Eleven Bagatelles*) by Erich Urbanner (Universal Edition).

Mother (from *A Child Loves*) by Darius Milhaud (Leeds Music Corporation).

No. 3 of *Six Rumanian Folk Dances* by Béla Bartók (Universal Edition 5802).

Allegretto (from *The New Piano Book*, Vol. III) by Philip Jarnach (Schott)

For conservative tastes:

    The Sea is Angry (No. 16 of *Five by Ten* Grade II) by William Alwyn (Lengnick).

    The Nightingale (No. 6 of *Andersen's Fairy Tales*, Op. 30) by Serge Bortkiewicz (Lengnick, Rahter).

GRADES V–VI

Sonatina No. 1 by Kenneth Leighton (Lengnick).
Sonatina in C Major, Op. 13 No. 1 by Kabalevsky (Boosey and Hawkes.)
No. III of *Impressiones Intimas* by Mompou (U.M.P.).
Selected pieces from *Pieces and Canons* by Eva Pain (Lengnick).

> No. 1 'A Primeval Forest'
> No. 2 'F major Canon'
> No. 3 'A Musical Ride'
> No. 5 'Idyll'
> No. 7 'A Mountain Stream'

GRADE VI

The Child that is born on The Sabbath Day (from *A Week of Birthdays*) by
Richard Rodney Bennett (Mills Music Ltd).
Prelude, Op. 34 No. 22 from *Twenty-four Preludes* by Shostakovich (Boosey
and Hawkes).
No. 1 of *Mouvements Perpetuels* by Poulenc (Chester).
No. 1 of *Six Rumanian Folk Dances* by Béla Bartók (Universal Edition 5802).
No. 1 of *Three Fantastic Dances*, Op. 1, by Shostakovich (Boosey and
Hawkes).
Chanson Antique and *By the Lake*, from *The Enchanted Trumpet* by Alfred
Nieman (Lengnick).

Selected pieces from *Five by Ten* Grade IV (Moderate to Moderately Difficult) (Lengnick).

> No. 6 Madeleine Dring, 'Nightfall'
> No. 7 Charles Proctor, 'Barcarolle'
> No. 8 Bernard Stevens, 'Nocturne No. 1'
> No. 9 Franz Reizenstein, 'Study in Accidentals'

GRADES VI–VII

Promenade from *A La Campagne* by John Tobin (Lengnick).
Selected pieces from *Little Suite of Rumanian Folk Dances* by Sabin V.
Drăgoi (Simrock edition 3053, Lengnick).

> No. 4 'Couple Dance from Bozovici'
> No. 5 'Folk Dance from Năsaŭd'
> No. 7 'Ring Dance from Năsaŭd'

No. 5 of *Six Rumanian Folk Dances* by Béla Bartók (Universal Edition 5082).
Pastourelle by Francis Poulenc (U.M.P.).
Secreto from *Impressiones Intimas* by Frederico Mompou (U.M.P.).

Dance Diversions for piano by M. Campbell Bruce (Curwen).

No. 3 of *Four Romantic Pieces for Piano* by Alan Rawsthorne (O.U.P.).

Basse-Danse and *Pieds-en-L'air* from *Capriol Suite* by Peter Warlock, arranged for Piano Solo by Maurice Jacobson (Curwen 99087).

GRADE VII

Tanzstück from *Das Neue Klavier-Buch* by Paul Hindemith (Schott).

Dance by Khachaturian, edited A. Rowley (Boosey and Hawkes).

Suite for Piano by Alfred Nieman (Lengnick).

The Sewing Machine (No. 7 of *Five by Ten* Grade V, Moderately Difficult to Difficult) by Elizabeth Maconchy (Lengnick).

Cunning Fox by Franz Reizenstein (No. 10 of the same).

Gavotta, Op. 32 No. 3, by Prokofiev (Boosey and Hawkes).

No. 6 of *Six Rumanian Folk Dances* by Béla Bartók (Universal Edition 5802)

Intermezzo 2 from *Les Ritournelles* by Bohuslav Martinů (Schott).

Nos. 2 and 3 of *Three Fantastic Dances* by Shostakovich, Op. 1 (Boosey and Hawkes).

Popular Song from *Façade* by William Walton, arranged by Roy Douglas (Oxford University Press).

GRADE VIII

No. 3 of *Mouvements Perpetuels* by Poulenc (Chester).

From the Diary of a Fly by Béla Bartók (*Mikrokosmos*, Vol. VI) (Boosey and Hawkes).

Toccata by Khachaturian (Boosey and Hawkes).

No. 1 of *Five Inventions*, Op. 14, by Bernard Stevens (Lengnick).

Six Preludes for Piano by Lennox Berkeley (Chester).

Five Bagatelles, Piano Solo, by Howard Ferguson (Boosey and Hawkes).

Second Sonata for Piano by Hindemith (Schott edition 2519).

4. AND ALL THAT JAZZ!

> 'There is too wide a gap between popular music on one side and classics on the other. Actually, the only thing that counts in music is whether it is good or bad.' Lawrence Tibbett.

Since the war it has become quite 'respectable' to admit to an interest in jazz. Earnest young men are very erudite about jazz-men and styles, and the Swingles have fun with Bach. You are more of 'a square' if you like it 'hot' than if you like it 'cool', and if you have just caught up with 'Trad' you are not yet 'with it'.

Amateur pianists are often frightened of spoiling their touch by attempting popular style playing—though large numbers of very serious organists continue to wage war on the piano keyboard in persistent attempts to push it through the floor! No one, however, dares to suggest to them that they should not 'mix it'.

Of those amateurs who would like to try their hand at jazz, etc., many do not know how to set about it. Most accredited piano teachers do not cater for this type of pupil. Incidentally, I was told of one in New Zealand who specialized in popular-style teaching, but who kept her 'method' a strict secret from other teachers!

The usual method of learning is to get to know someone who has the 'know-how', and to watch and listen to him. The other way is to buy records and to ape these. This is perhaps the most widely used means.

About nine years ago, however, the Middlesex County Council began looking into the possibility of providing Jazz classes in their educational establishments. And, largely owing to the pioneering work of Mr Owen Bryce, these are now available at Hendon Technical College, Chiswick Polytechnic, and Catford Evening Institute, Lewisham, where ensemble work is undertaken. Specific instruction in piano jazz, though, has still to come. Adult beginners could help to create a demand for this by badgering their own local authority. In the meantime the following publications should prove useful:[1]

Russ Henderson's *Popular Style Piano Playing:* Modern Keyboard Interpretation on a Harmonic Basis (Chappell).

> Part I. Sectionized Course with supplementary reference papers.
> Part II. Chord-Check Cards.
> Part III. Left Hand Rhythm.
> Part IV. Right Hand Treatments.
> Part V. Introductions and Endings.

Also from Chappell are three books by Jack Foy:

> *Pre-Pops* (An Introduction to popular Music for Piano).
> *Pop Stix* (Further Adventures in Popular Music for Piano).
> *Keyboard Pops* (Fourteen Pieces in Modern Popular Style).
> *Five in Jive* by Joseph W. Grant.

Keith Prowse feature publications by Billy Mayerl[2] whose *Special Tutor Course in Modern Syncopation* is quite well known. There are also 3 books of *Studies in Syncopation* by Mayerl; and 4 books of 3 pieces under the

---

[1] See also p. 59, Popular Style.
[2] The 'live' Billy Mayerl school is, I am informed, now closed down.

generic title *In my Garden* (I Springtime, II Summertime, III Autumntime, IV Wintertime). In a foreword to these Mr Mayerl writes, 1946: 'Syncopated music, in the sense of the word, has long been beyond the technical ability of the average amateur or beginner. . . . In writing these little pieces I have endeavoured to avoid all these difficulties without losing to any large degree the desired effect. There are no big stretches, the triplet and dotted quaver runs lie well under the fingers, accents are marked where best suited and "jumps" are entirely eliminated.

'Apart from their value as stepping stones to greater proficiency it is hoped that they will prove welcome additions to the repertoire of the piano student.'

Keith Prowse also publish Lee Sims' *Beginners' Piano Method* (*Jazz*) and Lee Sims' *Piano Method* (*Jazz*). Also three albums of easy syncopated solos —*Swingy Fingers*; *Here's Boogie Woogie*; and *Let's Go Latin American* by Stanford King.

Warren and Phillips publish George Coulter's *Short Syncopations for Pianoforte* (Miniatures in modern syncopated and rhythmic style playing kept within easy technical grasp, include Tango, Rag, Blues, etc.).

Ascherberg Hopwood and Crew publish *Easy-to-Play 'Beat' Book* by Ronnie Aldrich (Cha-cha, Rock 'n' Roll, etc.); *Beginners Play Boogie-Woogie* by Stuart Monroe; *Beginners Play Jazz* by Virgilio Piubeni.

Francis Day and Hunter publish *You can learn Jazz* by Freddy Clayton.

5. SOME VERY FIRST ALBUMS FOR THE ADULT BEGINNER

Two Keys to the Keyboard by Arthur Hollander (Keith Prowse). 'A Beginning Piano Method for the Adult or Teen-ager.'

'A new two-way approach incorporating simultaneous learning of Note Reading and "Chording" Songs and Playing by Ear.'

Adult Preparatory Piano Book by John Thompson (Chappell).

'It is designed especially for the Adult and its purpose is to lead the student quickly but thoroughly through the elements of piano study. At its conclusion the student may proceed to John Thompson's Second Grade Book and to continue thereafter in regular order with the succeeding books in his Modern Course for the Piano.'

Why Not Play the Piano? by Sidney Harrison (Boosey and Hawkes).

'This self-tutor is designed for anyone from 12 to 90. It shows you how to read, to play with rhythm, and to cultivate the actions that produce good sound. From small fragments of melody you are led, stage by stage, to a collection of complete pieces. Some are the simple tunes we all whistle and hum: some are the works of great masters. There are no baby pieces about teddy-bears.

'At the end of the book you will know whether it is worth your while to take lessons.'

The Adult Beginner, Vols. I and II, by Barbara Kirkby-Mason (Bosworth).
'With these books make use of First Album Part II and First Album Supplement (Bosworth) as extra material for Sight-Reading and for gaining confidence in the easier keys. As a Revision Course they may be used as reference books, as sight-reading material for pupils restarting lessons, as a means of revising scales and theory, and for self-help when lesson time is limited.'

Musical Beginnings for all at the Piano by Barbara Kirkby-Mason (Bosworth).
A de luxe edition with four-colour cover reproduction of Jan Vermeer's 'The Concert'. Includes very easy and attractive pieces of Early English Composers, with historical notes.

Adult Piano Course. Book I: *For the Adult Beginner* by John W. Schaum, followed by Books II and III (Bosworth).
'After Book III the Progressive succession of the "Adult Course" leads without the creation of a so called "gap" into Books "E", "F", "G", "H", of the John Schaum Piano Course.'

Adult Piano Course by Michael Aaron (Mills Music Ltd).
'A course designed to meet the demand for a piano method planned specifically for the teen-age and adult beginner, providing much useful teaching material in simple arrangements of well-known classical works, original and traditional pieces, and technical exercises.'

Better Beginnings by James Ching (Bosworth).
'A first book for everyone who wants to become a really good pianist and musician.'

Note. Also see *Pianophone Tuition Courses*, page 58.

6. FOR MOTHERS AND FATHERS TO PLAY TO THEIR CHILDREN

So many adults I have met have said: 'I'd give anything to be able to play the piano. If only my parents had made me practise when I was young!'

A parent's duty today, however, is not so much to 'put a child to piano lessons' and make him practise as to *arouse the child's own desire to learn*. In twenty years' time he will not then be lamenting: 'If only I had been made to practise': he will *want* to.

You can get your own young children interested in the piano and eager to learn if you will play to them from some of the many attractive albums available for the children of today. A sample selection of these is given below.

Easier than Easy by Ada Richter (U.M.P.).
Eighteen short pieces with words, illustrated in black and white.

A Day at the Farm by Eileen D. Robilliard (Chappell).
'Twelve very easy pieces for young children who are just beginning to play, illustrating a delightful little story.'

Ready Steady Go by Marjorie Heyler (Novello).
Twelve attractive pieces with delightful colour illustrations.

Toy-Box Suite by Barbara Kirkby-Mason (Curwen 8928).
Seven pieces with verses illustrating the true happenings of toys that really exist.

Enid Blyton Noddy Song Book No. 1 (Ricordi), Music by R. C. Noel Johnson.
'For singing, playing, acting, dancing and marching.'

Rupert Music Book No. 2 (Ascherberg), Music by Clive Mannering.
Contains two complete stories: 'Rupert and the Birthday Candles', and 'Rupert and the Glass Pool', with pictures in full colour. For playing, singing, marching and dancing.

The Oxford Nursery Song Book (O.U.P.).
Collected and arranged by Percy C. Buck, illustrated by Klara. Percy Buck writes: 'I have tried . . . to harmonize the tunes so that the ordinary mother or nurse, however small her piano technique, may be able to "keep things going".'

The Easiest Tune Book of Christmas Carols by E. Franklin-Pike (Ashdown).
'Twenty favourite carols which anyone can play. An absolute boon for the fireside or school. Words and music for each item. The harmony has a very full and satisfying quality although there are only single notes in each hand.'

At Christmastide and *In Nursery-Rhyme Land* by Barbara Kirkby-Mason (Bosworth) contain very simple piano solos and duets with words and some recorder parts. Both have charming reproduction picture covers.

Highwayman Dick (A Romantic Suite for Piano) by Clive Harty (Walsh Holmes).

Twelve scenes from Hiawatha by Stanley Wilson (Forsyth).
Each piece is prefixed by a quotation from the poem.

Robin Hood by Leslie Fly (Forsyth).

Twelve musical pieces illustrating scenes in the life of Robin Hood and his merry men.

Pantomime People by Thomas Arnold Johnson (Lengnick).

Six characteristic pieces with preliminary exercises for each piece.

Children's Zoo by John Lanchbery (Curwen).

Twelve musicianly little pieces, good for developing a sense of interpretation. 10-year-olds will enjoy them.

London Holiday by John Longmire (Freeman).

Seven easy miniatures by a composer who knows how to attract children to music.

Alice in Wonderland by E. Markham Lee (O.U.P.). Twelve Easy Duets for Pianoforte, in two books.

Very imaginative, and really good musical fun.

7. HOW TO WIN FRIENDS . . .
(Or 'Showing off'—in a nice way!)

The following pieces either *sound* much more difficult than they are to play, or are simply written but with adult appeal, and call for interpretative rather than technical prowess. The grading is from the beginning to just beyond the 'Half-way' standard, and some popular light pieces and piano arrangements of orchestral works are included.

PRELIMINARY—GRADE I

A Spanish Fiesta. Page 63, John Thompson's *Adult Preparatory Piano Book* (Chappell).

Boogie at Midnight, from *Pre-Pops* by Jack Foy (Chappell). Very easy to memorize.

Habanera from Carmen. Page 66, John Thompson's *Modern Course for the Piano*, 2nd Grade Book (Chappell).

Tango. No. 1 of Latin American Dances by June Weybright (Willis Music Company).

Bolero. No. 2 of the above.

That Cuban Conga Chain, from *Let's go Latin American* by Stanford King (Keith Prowse).

Sur la glace à Sweet Briar by C. H. Crawford (Mills Music Ltd). 'Showy' piece based on arpeggio figures, very easy to memorize.

From Brazil (No. 19); *From Ireland* (No. 16); *From Belgium* (No. 17); of
Round the World Book 2 by James Easson (Curwen 5135).
Attractive piano settings of folk tunes.

From Erin. No. 3 of *A Little Suite* by Felix Swinstead (Short Original
Pieces for Piano, Associated Board). Haunting cantabile right-hand
melody with very simple chordal accompaniment.

Easy on the Eyes, from *Keyboard Pops* by Jack Foy (Chappell). Introduces
characteristic dotted crotchet quaver figure of 'pop' music.

Dolly's Funeral. No. 7 of *Album for the Young*, Op. 39 by Tchaikovsky. It
doesn't *sound* at all childish!

GRADES II–III

Minuet in D Minor by J. S. Bach from *A Little Notebook for Anna Magdalena
Bach.* No. 18 in the Associated Board edition.

Prelude in C Minor by J. S. Bach. No. 3 of *12 Short Preludes*, various publishers.

Corranto in A Minor from *Easy Elizabethans* (O.U.P.).

Bourrée, Shore's Trumpet, Saraband, and *Air for the Flutes* from *When Anne
was Queen,* suite for piano by Alec Rowley (Ashdown).

Siciliana by Harold Rutland (O.U.P.).

Douce Plainte. Study in G Minor, Op. 100 No. 16, by Burgmüller (Augener).

Ballade. Study in C Minor, as above, No. 15.

First Loss by Schumann from *Album for the Young*, Op. 68 No. 16.

A Sad Moment by Ivor Foster from *Classic and Romantic Pieces* Grade II
(Associated Board).

A Celtic Song by Thomas Dunhill (Associated Board).

Song by Candelight, No. 6 of *Round the Clock* by Margaret Lyell (Curwen).

To a Wild Rose, Op. 51 No. 1, by E. Macdowell (Elkin).

Spiritual from *Jardin d'Enfants* by Jean Wiener (U.M.P.).

Rhythm and Blues and *Lazy Louie* from *Pre-Pops* by Jack Foy (Chappell).

Jus' Noodlin and *Slow Rock'n' Roll*, from *Keyboard Pops* by Jack Foy (Chappell).

Frisco Fog, from *Pop Stix* by Jack Foy (Chappell).

Maracas in Caracas and *Girl with a Fan* (Tango), from *Let's go Latin American*
by Stanford King (Keith Prowse).

Theme from Z Cars (Johnny Todd) by Bridget Fry. Arranged for Piano
Solo from the B.B.C. series (Essex Music Ltd).

The Maigret Theme by Ron Grainer. From the B.B.C. Inspector Maigret
series (Manette Music Co, Ltd).

The Third Man (The Harry Lime Theme) based on music composed and
arranged by Anton Karas (Chappell).

A Legend of Nazareth No. 4, and *Chanson Triste* No. 1, from *Tchaikovsky Album* arranged by Heller Nicholls (Warren and Phillips).

Elizabethan Serenade by Ronald Binge (Ascherberg, Hopwood and Crew).

A Lonely Bird, No. 4 of *Country Sketches* by Cecil Baumer (Elkin).

White Landscape by Rose Thurlow (Curwen 93381).

Cherry Blossom from *In my Garden*, I Springtime, by Billy Mayerl (Keith Prowse). Easy syncopated, but typical Mayerl style.

Forgotten Dreams, Piano Solo by Leroy Anderson (Mills Music Ltd). Used as a signature tune for one of B.B.C.'s Woman's Hour romantic serials.

Stardust Falls, and *Broken Hearted*, from *Keyboard Pops* by Jack Foy (Chappell). Popular 'ballad' style.

Jamaican Rumba, the well-known piano solo by Arthur Benjamin (Boosey and Hawkes).

Eighteenth Variation from Rhapsody on a Theme of Paganini by S. Rachmaninoff, adapted for piano solo by Eichhorn (Schott). Source of music of 'The Story of Three Loves'.

The Messiah. Melodies from Handel's oratorio easily arranged for the pianoforte by Noel Fisher (Hinrichsen).

Twenty Symphony Melodies, easily arranged for pianoforte by Thomas A. Johnson (Weekes).

Themes from the Great Concertos, easily arranged for pianoforte by Thomas A. Johnson (Warren and Phillips).

Themes from Well Known Violin Concertos, easily arranged for pianoforte by Thomas A. Johnson (Weekes).

Twelve Melodies of the Ballet, easily arranged for pianoforte by Thomas A. Johnson (Weekes).

Theme from Piano Concerto (Schumann) arranged for Piano Solo by Henry Duke (Freeman).

Excerpts from Concertos played by Eileen Joyce arranged for Piano Solos by Victor Ambroise (Lawrence Wright).

Beethoven Concerto No. 3 in C Minor, Op. 37, arranged for Piano Solo by Noel Fisher (Peters Edition No. 2894cc. Moderately Difficult).

Beethoven Concerto No. 4 in G Major, Op. 58, arranged for Piano Solo by Noel Fisher (Peters Edition No. 2894dd. Abridged Version. Moderately Difficult).

Beethoven Concerto No. 5 (Emperor), as above, No. 2894ee.

Schumann Concerto in A Minor, Op. 54, as above, No. 2898a.

Grieg Concerto in A Minor, Op. 16, arranged for Piano Solo by Wilhelm Weismann (Peters Edition No. 2164b. Moderately Difficult).

Tchaikovsky Concerto No. 1 in B flat Minor, Op. 23, arranged for Piano Solo by Noel Fisher (Peters Edition No. 3775a. Moderately Difficult).

Rachmaninoff Second Piano Concerto, Op. 18, simplified and abridged edition by E. Thorne from *Favourite Piano Pieces of Today* (Boosey and Hawkes). This book contains nine items including the Serenade from *Hassan* by Delius, and arrangements of the March from *Peter and the Wolf* by Prokofiev, and of *La Calinda* by Delius—all rather more difficult than the Rachmaninoff, but worth knowing about.

Franck, Symphonic Variations, abridged version for Piano Solo arranged by Noel Fisher (Peters Edition No. 3741a. Moderately Difficult).

Fantasia on Greensleeves by R. Vaughan Williams, adapted from the Opera 'Sir John in Love', arranged for pianoforte solo (Oxford University Press). Moderately Difficult.